S0-ABR-991

FAITH BALDWIN

Cuthrell

Evening Star

WITHDRAWN

966943

HOLT,
RINEHART AND WINSTON
NEW YORK   CHICAGO
SAN FRANCISCO

Copyright © 1964, 1965, 1966 by Faith Baldwin Cuthrell

All rights reserved, including the right to reproduce
this book or portions thereof in any form.

Published simultaneously in Canada by Holt, Rinehart and
Winston of Canada, Limited.

Library of Congress Catalog Card Number: 66-25593

Some of the material in this book has appeared previously
in *Woman's Day*.

First Edition

Designer: Ernst Reichl
80793-1416
Printed in the United States of America

This book is for
The New Canaan Book Shop

*with love and gratitude to Elizabeth
Young and Edith Rees, who preside over
it; and it is also for all those who
serve therein, temporarily or permanently,
in order to make friends and strangers
feel happy and at home.*

Foreword

Why I write forewords to all my nonfiction books and even to some of my novels, I don't know. Perhaps it is because I was, in my youth, accustomed to reading books older than I, which usually had a short exhortation addressed to Gentle Reader. (Those writers were optimists.) And perhaps, consciously or not, it's by way of explanation and apology. Anyway, any reader, gentle or otherwise, has the privilege of skipping them.

Where shall I begin this time? One inflexible rule—there used to be one, I know—is that a book should have a beginning, a middle, and an end. This seems reasonable.

I have been forced, reluctantly, to look at my five previous books of nonfiction (I don't read my own books, once published, unless something is reprinted after twenty or thirty years, and I'm curious to know what it's about, having forgotten). However, in this case, it seemed that I should know where the other five had started.

Two, with the month of December; two, with the month of November, and one, with the month of October.

Now, proper or orthodox almanac-type books, also proper or orthodox journals and diaries begin boldly with January first, thus turning over the proverbial new leaf. I can only conclude that my little almanac-journals are—if not improper—then unorthodox.

Me, too.

Our calendar begins a new year with January first, too, but it has long seemed to me that we begin a new year— even a new era—every day of our lives. And a great many dates can signify a personal new year: one's birthday, for instance; Easter—in fact, almost any date in spring; Thanksgiving, because we look back in gratitude and ahead in trust; and, of course, Christmas, the giving time.

Thinking it over, I remember that the Chinese New Year does not fall upon the first of January; nor does the Russian or the Jewish.

I believe that September is a good month in which to start an almanac, a journal, or a journey. Summer is still with us much of the month, and autumn waits, a little way off, to warn us with light frost and turning leaves, bestowing cool nights as opposed to September's warm—well, usually warm—days.

So, we'll start with September.

Because I have called this small book *Evening Star,* many people will immediately think of Alfred Lord Tennyson's:

> Sunset and evening star,
> And one clear call for me!

But I didn't have this in mind.

Sunset in September isn't early, you know; not in my state where we have Daylight Saving until late October. And September isn't really a downhill month; it's more of a plateau between the summer slopes and the slow climb up winter's hill. Moreover, I haven't as yet heard the

8

"clear call" meant by Tennyson. Just a whisper now and then, perhaps—and while it is true that I'm in the autumnal and sunset years, to say nothing of having passed the Biblical three score and ten, I can't hold with the theory that these are "the days of our years." Geriatrics— or the practices of this medical science—appear to have lengthened the average life span; sometimes for better; sometimes, I fear, for worse. Insurance tables show that both men and women are living longer, barring, of course, accidents, wars, and other violent deaths.

One of my grandmothers lived to be, I think, over sixty. But the other was eighty-five before she left us; her daughter, my mother, was eighty-five also, but my father was only fifty-eight.

It's hard to average up if you believe in ancestral longevity as the clue to your own. How could I, with an aunt dying in her thirties, and her sister, twelve days short of one hundred?

So the evening star hasn't any special significance for me except that I love it. I like to see the morning star, too, if ever I'm up until it rises, or if I awaken at the time it does (both of which are unlikely). But the morning star is pale in the predawn sky and the evening star is bright as polished silver.

Will you come with me on a brief journey through a year? . . . I've put more than one month into any given one; and I'm planning to travel for thirteen months, as I have before, because it's pleasant to write about a month I've not yet lived. Besides, unlike most people, I think that thirteen is a lucky number!

So let us explore a little within this house and outside of it, in other states than mine, and in other countries not recently revisited by me, except in memory. We can observe the morning star, the rising and setting sun, the

9

clouds, the darkness and the storms, which are all part of the pattern; and never forget the evening star which is to me a symbol of guidance through the night, whether it be moonless or not.

What was it Macdonald Clarke wrote?

> Whilst twilight's curtain spreading far,
> Was pinned with a single star.

For me this will be a journey backwards and forwards in time; for you, an armchair excursion. As the Apocrypha says, "God . . . prosper your journey. . . ."

F. B.

Evening Star

September

"Up from the meadows rich with corn
Clear in the cool September morn . . ."

JOHN GREENLEAF WHITTIER

In this poem, which almost every school child has read, Mr. Whittier was talking about Maryland, and also about Barbara Frietchie. There's no corn growing in my fields, but under one of the apple trees as we go down the slope toward the duck pond, my patriarch woodchuck is sitting in meditation. He has one of the last of the August apples in his hands and now and then he takes a thoughtful bite. He's been around all summer, but I see him more often during this month.

September is a remembering sort of month, halfway between here and there, and sometimes the mornings are not as cool as in Mr. Whittier's poem.

It is also the back-to-school month and my grandchildren are returning to their various schools. I appear to have them in almost all grades. This is also the time when

13

they have grown out of last year's fall clothes and shoes. For most grownups, too, vacations are over and the preoccupied, pressed life begins all over again.

A few leaves have turned by early September. Tell me, why does one make up its mind to light a tiny golden or scarlet flame while hundreds of others on the same tree decide to remain green and wait a little longer?

The first flash of color always excites me as much as the first frail, courageous bloom of spring. This is, in a sense, my season—sometimes warm and, when the wind blows an alert, sometimes cold. But there is a clarity about September. On clear days, the sun seems brighter, the sky more blue, the white clouds take on marvelous shapes; the moon is a wonderful apparition, rising gold, cooling to silver; and the stars are so big. The September storms—the hurricane warnings far away, the sudden gales, the downpour of rain that we have so badly needed here for so long—are exhilarating, and there's a promise that what September starts, October will carry on, catching the torch flung into her hand.

The other night I was alone and watching television upstairs on the sun porch. Perhaps I should call it the Florida room, but it isn't in Florida. I had just watered my African violets—poor things, so generous with blossom when I give them so little, and such ignorant, care—and the begonias, and I remembered that other begonias and the gardenia plant, which are outdoors, must soon be brought inside. I turned off the set and the light above it and sat there in the big shabby rocking chair to look out at the far reaches of a sky which was, that night, starless. It was very quiet in the old house and only now and then could I hear a passing car or the sound of a plane and see its light like a different kind of star tracking across the heavens.

14

Such moments, spent in solitude and stillness, bring us very close to God, I think, to nature, and to all the wonders which lie around us and which, in our hurrying hours, we forget to ponder upon.

Sitting there, I reflected upon the sights and sounds of many years, some of which can break the heart with nostalgia and others which lift the aspiring spirit.

Hundreds come easily to mind; others, painfully. Many repeat themselves in actuality year in and year out, if with variations; some I'll never see or hear again except in memory. But each is really a collector's item.

The mind is like a television screen and pictures continually flow across it: pictures from long ago, from far away, from yesterday, or near at hand, and even—imagined—from tomorrow. On the screen of memory there are often faces I've not seen for years in the flesh and others which I see almost every day; all dear to me, hence never to be forgotten.

There are also places, and when I think of those I've known, I am there instantly, for thought travels faster than the swiftest plane man has built or ever will build. I may be sitting on the sun porch on a quiet evening, but thought can take me instantly to a spot where I can sit under the Hawaiian sun and look at Diamond Head; or I can walk through a London street in the rain, or go into the great cathedral of St. Paul's and sit quietly there, or climb the many stairs to the top to look over the vast city.

I shall never tire of remembering Diamond Head, which I've seen countless times. It is part of my collection, one of the reels for my screen forever, and no matter what they do on the island of Oahu in the way of building and progress, they can never, I trust, spoil it—never, anyway, for me, for I always see it as first I saw it. I will never tire, either, of my reel of St. Paul's, which I've seen only twice

15

from the inside. Here in this house I have actual pictures: in my bedroom an attractive old English post card, framed, of St. Paul's; in the living room the painting, done for me by a friend, of Diamond Head as she saw it from her own house back in 1942.

In numerous places there are lonely beaches and wind-carved dunes, high mountains, rolling hills, which at any moment I can throw upon my screen.

Sounds are also collector's items; these live mostly in the inner ear: voices I haven't heard for a long time; the sound of a small organ being played by someone I love—he used to play "Home on the Range" in his limited, half-learned, half-by-ear repertory. Sometimes I can remember my father's marvelous speaking voice, and sometimes the voices of great singers, now silenced on this earth.

Every year there are sounds which repeat themselves: the first peepers in spring, high, bell-like, lonely, but hopeful. And another lonely sound which some people dislike, but which I love, is the call of an owl, unseen, hooting from a nearby tree. But then I have an affinity for owls.

I used to hate the sound of train whistles, or the barks of a diesel engine when I lived closer to the railroads than now. They made me restless; they were lonely, as are foghorns and the buoy bell, in the night.

Bird song, timid and heartening, in early spring; the unmistakable call of the red-winged blackbird, the cardinal whistling in the snow, the intrepid questioning of the chickadee—these are memorable sounds; one never wearies of them and each year, in the proper season, they are renewed.

Unless it happens to be a leaking faucet, I've always loved the sound of water, the sea sliding silkily upon the sands, or coming in, roaring and crested, to crash against

16

the rocks. On Cape Cod I hear it often at night; sometimes it sounds like a freight train, of all things.

I know the voices of the rivers around New York and Brooklyn, and the sound of the St. Lawrence, lapping in quietude, or in storm speaking with anger.

Helen Hokinson once lived near a brook; always, anywhere in her house you could hear it talking to itself.

My own brook rarely says a word except after melting ice and spring rain or the autumn storms. Lately it's been perfectly mute. Because of the drought these many moons there's scarcely a drop of water in it. Oh, a little in spring and fall, but in summer it is as a fountain sealed (which reminds me that I also have fountains). In any case, in order to hear my brook, even when it's in voice, you have to walk down toward it; it's too distant from the house for any chatter to reach you; and although I am not far from Long Island Sound, I'm too far to hear what it has to say and I can see it only in small, miragelike glimpses when the leaves are off the trees and I'm at an upstairs window.

There are sounds I do not like, but often hear: the incessant barking of dogs at night; the terrible screams of a trapped animal; the whine of a power saw, strong and petulant; and the sound of heavy traffic. Most city sounds afflict me, but other people listen to their so-called symphony as if the noise were music; as indeed it is, to them. I have had city people visit me in the country and complain about the quiet keeping them awake.

Sometimes I become somewhat incensed with katydids and locusts and other vocal insects when they insist upon serenading me all night. Yet, in a way, I like it.

There is music I love, some great, some small; there are certain songs which take me back in time. I can think of two at this moment, but I can't carry a tune, so they

17

have to sing in my inner ear, which is as true as the outer is false. These two songs I can hardly bear to hear, even privately, yet I listen to them and sometimes even ask for them when a real orchestra is playing and there are others beside myself to listen.

In a lifetime we see and hear innumerable things. We have countless records stacked in the attic of memory; some are lost or broken or thrown away, but others can play for us clearly and with meaning.

In this era we find ourselves haunted by phrases and catch words. Some are short-lived, others become part of the language. We all use them, even if some of us don't wholly comprehend their meaning. Nowadays everything has to be "in depth"; and it wasn't so long ago that the word "status" took on a highly polished sheen, passing, as it did, and still does, through everyone's idle conversation. And then, of course, there's the "frame of reference," a phrase which, when first I heard it, puzzled me. But there's one thing of which I'm certain—we can remember "in depth" or just skim the surface like a dragonfly.

Do you dream in color? I often do. I remember in color also: the black beaches of Hawaii, the pink beaches of Florida and Bermuda, the fine cream white sand of some seashores and the coarser brown and gray sand of others.

Nowadays, I'm forgetful—perhaps I always was. But forgetfulness increases with one's years, perhaps because we unconsciously try to lighten our burden. I forget telephone numbers, engagements, gloves, handbags, and what I had for dinner last night—and often, alas, names. But there are people, places, vistas, and sounds which will be with me as long as memory remains. We're told that actually we never forget anything, not one tiny thing we've heard or seen throughout our lives; that everything

18

lives on in the unconscious. It's a rather sobering and alarming thought.

We're told that animals remember, and we've all had proof that they do, though much of their remembering is connected with the scent of a place, a room, a person. Some of our memories, too, are awakened by scent, but only man remembers with clarity on other levels. When we least expect it, something seen, heard, or experienced five, ten, even fifty years ago, comes back to us, evoked by something we see, hear or read, or, quite without recognizable evocation, it's there, as sudden as summer lightning.

We are blessed with so many God-given qualities: thought, reason, free will, memory, and above all, the quality of being able to give and receive love.

Gussie just came in as I was writing this and bade me come and look at Grandpa Woodchuck. He's right there under the apple tree. Few August windfalls remain, and the birds seem to eat those, too. Hasn't Mr. Woodchuck learned, I wonder, to try the crab apples from our one such tree, or to go into the far fields where there are still older trees and later apples? I think he's in a rut.

Though the summer theaters have closed their doors, I look back upon a pleasant season in nearby Westport, where I went, whenever I could, with my friend Alma. Last year I went to our own Stratford for some Shakespeare, but this past summer I missed the theater by the river and the fine performances.

Did you know that the first known performance of Shakespeare in America was back in 1737 in Charleston? I didn't until I read *Will Shakespeare and His America,* by my friends Nancy and Jean Webb, the first book written about Shakespearian performances in America—

where and when and by whom. How pleasant that we discovered Mr. Shakespeare so long ago, though it was really one hundred and twenty-one years after his death!

Never mind that the summer theaters have closed, for what is more scenically perfect, more brilliantly cast, and dramatic than the turning of the leaves, early autumn's own trooping of the colors? I often ask myself why I endure the winters hurled upon us by this climate—to say nothing of some of the more uncomfortable summers—and then I reply to myself that the inconvenience and discomfort are negligible in comparison with the delight of coasting from summer into autumn, from winter into spring.

Now that we are exploring Outer Space, wondering about climates, conditions, and possible life on other planets, not to mention the moon, I am certain that, unless they ultimately discover a planet which is twin to our own, I'll prefer to remain here, where the orderly procession of the seasons takes place and where, in every season, even in a New England winter or the humid spells of summer there is a familiar, yet altering enchantment.

Most of my birthday-card sending is behind me for this month. September in my family is an anniversary month, that of my older son and his wife, Janet; it was also that of my parents. Not long ago a friend wrote me she had a spoon from the first Chicago World's Fair, and shortly before her letter came I'd seen reproduced on television a tiny corner of that Fair of 1892 . . . and remembered that my parents, on their September wedding journey, had visited the Fair. (At their hotel, they borrowed a friend's child to sit at table with them lest they be thought bride and groom.)

It's difficult to think of people you know only as adults

20

as ever having been children, and young. How giant-sized they seemed when you were little. Then, as you grew up and watched your own children advance from infancy to childhood and then to maturity, it was still hard, but not impossible, to remember them as very young. But one's parents, that's another story. Yet, when I was a child, how young they were.

Every day in my blue and white bedroom with the dark exposed beams and the wide board floors, I look at pictures which hang to the right of my dressing table, one of a solemn young man at seventeen—he grew up to be my father; and the other of a pretty girl at sixteen—she became my mother. And now I try to place them a dozen or so years later, together, and at a World's Fair.

Now and again, despite the calendar and the leaves intent upon attaining glory, I think it's spring when I hear a bird sing nearby. It's cooler, they've come out of their hiding places and are getting together to decide where they'll spend the winter. Or I look out and see the migrants, passing through, pausing just long enough to enjoy a little snack at the feeders or snatch a few berries from a bush. I don't know where they're going, but they're on their way. My resident birds haven't started south as yet, and even next month there will still be robins. Some who like it here won't go away at all; they must have grown accustomed to this motel. But migrants are always as unexpected and exciting as the first turning leaf.

Each year at the beginning of a season's alteration I pause to consider the Plan which made it so. Even in climates we think of as fixed—subtropic or tropic—there are really seasons. They are not as marked as ours here, but they include great rains and wild winds, all sorts of disturbances and fluctuations of temperature as well as great beauty.

21

I've always been interested in plans, but I can't read a blueprint. I've never been able to "see" a house or a room when it's just on paper. I remember when Gladys Taber was about to add the beautiful wing on the Cape Cod House. I was there and saw the plans. I also saw the space staked out and even some of the great machinery move in to chew up the earth. But I couldn't believe that between those stakes and from that excavation the wing would one day rise.

I like other kinds of plans, too. Many of mine do not materialize, but half the fun is the blueprint in our minds and dreams. And I like to hear other people's plans whether or not they turn out as originally designed. But the plans of nature, the unswerving stars, the meteors and comets, the rising and setting of sun and moon, the migration of birds, the hibernation of some animals, and the diligent endeavors of squirrels and chipmunks to provide for a day in which food will not be plentiful—these have always fascinated me.

The plans of mankind, the over-all blueprint for living and world betterment, so far have fallen all too short of the goal . . . perhaps someday they will be achieved, even if only in part.

But the Great Plan is, of course, that which has guided all creation since the very beginning.

Often I hear people say of their own or someone else's problem, "It will work out." I've said it myself. And it's true. Often things don't work out quite as desired, but work out they do in the long run. This is something to keep in mind, and to hold fast.

Last spring, when my older daughter and her husband were looking for a house, they found one they thought was right, and after they'd looked at wallpapers and taken measurements, crawling around baseboards, they discovered it wasn't. I thought she'd be crushed, and offered a word of sympathy, but she said, "Well, it's a disappointment, but we'll go on looking—something's bound to turn up, and better. It will work out."

It did. I saw their new place—it's old, really—early last summer. Gussie and I went up. My daughter, having broken her wrist almost as soon as she moved, was not able to cater to a couple of guests, so we brought a picnic-type lunch, and stayed until the children came home from school. It's quite a house; it has ten acres, a river, and lovely trees, and it's so quiet you can hear yourself thinking. Much will have to be done to it, of course; meantime, it's perfectly livable and lovely, and they're young, that family; they have time.

I've learned by now that—although my own plans may be suddenly changed, or I think I haven't time to do all I must do in a given period, or I get bogged down in the writing of a book and (unlike the migrant birds) have no idea where I'm going, or a sudden catastrophe crashes into the lives of those I love—it will all somehow, sometime, work out because in the Plan it always does.

Speaking of altered personal plans, a year ago August, I thought I was bound for Cape Cod. I wasn't. I was bound for the hospital instead. So, I went to the Cape in October. This year my thoughts turned Capeward in August, but I didn't go; my hostess had altered plans. But my daughter-in-law, Janet, and her children came to me from Florida for about five days. After that I had a brief illness and developed an allergy to the drug that cured it. Later I was granted an unexpected delightful weekend in the Berkshires with friends. Wonderful old house, wonderful old acres, mountains all about, and trees showing scarlet slashes. I slept in a bedroom which had once been a living room and had been left untouched,

23

except for the addition of sleeping accommodations. Who else, I wondered, has ever slept in a bedroom that had a fireplace, wing chairs, a million books, and a piano? How I wished that I could play; it would have pleased me to rise in the night and thunder out a bit of Brahms or Beethoven. After all, I was quite a distance from the other people in the house.

So when did I go to the Cape?

When, but this very month, before the middle of it, when the goldenrod was out and the purple asters and the cranberry bogs were starting to turn. And we had hot and cold weather; we saw friends and talked half the nights away and listened to strange birds crying. I met some new friends, including a very new baby, and had a marvelous holiday, as I always do with Gladys. I came back home on the last day of this month . . . in time to be a year older.

In summer I observe fireflies—light without heat; during this month and next I watch the leaves—flames without fire.

My favorite modern song, one I love, yet sometimes weep to hear, is "The September Song." This has been a singing month, this September, and whatever has been inharmonious in it—for in every month there are times of discordance—I've already forgotten.

"As the Italians say, Good company in a journey make the way to seem shorter."

IZAAK WALTON

And I had thought, until I chanced upon this quotation, that he wrote mostly of fishing!

24

Well, if you are still with me, good companionship I'll have, and the time expended in writing this little book will seem shorter. But even if I'm alone with my typewriter, and without a potential reader looking over my shoulder, I'll be companioned, nevertheless. For work in itself is a partner; and I can think of past readers I've met—somewhere, anywhere, even through the mails—and of people who unconsciously assist me to write, as I remember their social qualities and the lessons I have learned from them.

This is a skyward journey, a journey toward the evening star; perhaps to the day star also. In the physical sense we go down the path from September toward October. In another sense we travel together the world over; even to those parts of it that I have never seen but somehow know because friends who have been there tell me of them; and there are motion pictures and television programs set against backgrounds unfamiliar to me, and books I can read, and photographs I can look at. Last summer I helped my sister put into albums a number of photographs she had taken in Spain and Portugal, and regarding each I was momentarily there.

In the pauses between work, outside engagements, and the arrivals and departures of friends and relatives, I take little trips in books. When my friends at the bookshop are in despair because I've read all the new mysteries, they send me novels, many of which I might never have read—I am no devotee of the so-called modern novel, generally speaking—except that they've been sent me. Sometimes, as for instance today when there are no new books in the house (and I've read most of the older ones I own several times, sometimes more often), I turn to books I haven't read for years.

Dickens, for instance. As a child in my father's library

25

I read through the whole set—everyone had sets in those days—and was repelled by most of them; bored with the length, the interminable descriptions and revolted by many of the characters, a reaction to which the illustrations contributed. By the time a little Dickens, beyond the *Christmas Carol,* was required reading in school, I skimmed through an assignment and said privately, "I can't stand Dickens."

My mother never could either except *The Tale of Two Cities,* at which my father, a passionate lover of the *Pickwick Papers,* used to remark that if you liked that, you didn't really like Dickens.

When I was in my early thirties, I decided to see if my taste had changed, at which point I bought myself a set of Dickens.

Other sets I've owned at one time or another have long since gone: my set of George Bernard Shaw, for instance, of Kipling and so on, given for the most part to my children. I still have all the volumes of Proust and hope someday to be able to read them with understanding; so far I haven't succeeded; and of *The Tale of Genji,* which occasionally I pick up, finding that I can understand these stories, despite their wholly exotic setting, antiquity, and their depiction of modes and manners wholly alien to us.

Anyway I'm back on Dickens again, for a little while. When I'm home, I read during my tray luncheon, and for a time before dinner if there are no guests, and often, in the evenings, on the sun porch when I prefer to have the voice of the television silent.

So now with Charles Dickens I'm making a journey—it will be interrupted, of course, but I'll return to it—through a London, an England, of a different era.

All reading matter, fiction or nonfiction, inspirational

or factual—no matter where the stage is set, whether the books were printed a hundred or more years ago or only yesterday, whether or not we like what we read—is a journey for the mind. We find ourselves in strange countries and walk in them with strange people, for a time. Often we do not like what we see and hear and encounter; often we do not comprehend it. It's like arriving someplace at night, and then in the morning looking out of the windows, not understanding what we see.

However, whether we travel with pleasure or repulsion, comprehension or bewilderment, these journeys expand the mind and enlarge our grasp of the world that once was or that which is now, or even that which may sometime be.

This journey I have invited you to undertake with me is through many years in retrospect, and through the present. You will meet some of my friends in the course of it . . . friends in and out of books; friends I see often, or hardly ever; friends I haven't seen for many years or shall not, in this lifetime, see again. You will wander through my house and my mind—I am afraid my house is the neater—share my dreams and look with me at the world outside and at the stars.

As to whether you will journey with me through the outer and inner space of myself, I do not know, for, to be honest with you, I do not believe that I, held back by ignorance or alarm, have explored it very deeply.

October

"Bright October was come, the misty-bright October."

ARTHUR HUGH CLOUGH

This month can produce blue-ribbon days; in fact, it's doing so right now; and last October when I was on Cape Cod it also obliged with a blue-ribbon sky and sea, fringed with golden sun against a spectacular back drop of scarlets, reds and golds—drought notwithstanding.

I don't understand drought anyway; with trees dying and lawns almost nonexistent and everyone saving water like crazy (me, too; how do I know when my well will go dry?) we had, in this section, and others the best apple crop in years!

Our New York World's Fair has closed. I didn't see it. My grandchildren did, and my sister, her grandchildren, and most of my friends. Oh, well, as I've said, my parents saw the Chicago one in '92 and with Mignon and Alan

Eberhart, I had a couple of glimpses of the much later spectacle in Chicago—a city of which I'm very fond but, then, I'm fond of many cities—and in 1939 on my way to Australia, I was in San Francisco and saw the Exposition on Treasure Island. I've never forgotten the flowers. When I returned home in August, the New York Fair was in full swing and my children regarded me with superiority. They'd been. So I went to that one under their guidance.

I remember my father telling me how, as a little boy right off the ship that brought him home from China, he went alone to a fair in Philadelphia. Or was it an exposition? . . . And when I was going on eight, he and mother saw the Pan-American Exposition in Buffalo. But my own first fair was in St. Louis.

It seems to me that the underlying value, one might even say spirit, of any great public spectacle has been overlooked by critics and admirers alike. Every one talks about what there is to see—of architecture and exhibitions; of lights and fountains; of the marvels of science, past, present, and future; and—in a less exalted key—of tired feet. But few seem to recognize, beyond the statistical figures involved, the presence of people from all over the world, for the most part in a unity of thought. This is not to say they agree on what's to see or hear or do, or that all remain serene under the pressure of crowds and tensions of confusion. But they are brought together with a single purpose: they have come to look, to wonder, and then depart; and they will have spoken to strangers; they will have shared.

I had a sharing experience one spring in a church not far away from me, where I spoke to a group of women (I was sorry for the two men present, the minister of the church and a young rabbi from our town). In that gathering there were members of two branches of

29

the Protestant church and of the Temple, the lovely name of which is Shalom, which means peace. And there were Negroes and white.

I've spoken before at interfaith and interracial meetings, but this one was special. There was within the group a lovely warmth, a sincere friendliness, and a sense of sharing. As I left with Gussie, who had driven me there, I thought: Sharing is the road to understanding, and only understanding is the way to peace.

We have so little, really; we never fully understand those closest to us—let alone strangers—or ourselves. But the seeking for comprehension, the search for understanding is a step upon the journey.

If you look back, as I do, upon the people you've known, well or slightly—briefly or for a long time—and contemplate your differences, your angers or frustrations, one with the other, even your estrangements and unhappiness, you will, I think, see that what was lacking in the relationships was understanding—which is not a one-way street. Sometimes, perhaps, we are afraid to understand lest our own weaknesses be exposed to us.

The great minds, which from time to time have existed in this world, were like doors thrown wide to understanding. I don't mean just their brilliance or philosophy or even psychology. I mean that the spoken words that have endured are those uttered by men who understood with their hearts.

No one on earth understands everything; that all-comprehensive function belongs to God alone. But we all try to understand a little. Most of us realize that too late. We look back and think: If only I'd tried to understand. Many failures in human relationships derive from this common failure.

Watching the birds flock to discuss their travels among

the brilliant leaves, listening to the slow turning of the earth upon her axis, meditating on Nature herself, never uncertain no matter how uncertain her manifestations may be, I think of the instinct that sends the birds from one locality to another, of the lengthening shadows as we face toward autumn, and of the marvelous system that encourages the leaf to fall and nurture the soil. In the singing flame of October it begins the lullaby that will put the roots of grass and flowers to sleep. This system, in the four definite seasons of my little world, will cover the ground with silent snow, and at a later date will shout that spring is coming and awaken sleepers to new life.

The sun in his glory, the moon in her phases, the stars in their courses, all these are part of the system; and Nature, turning the wheel of the seasons, understands what she must accomplish.

Each in our own way, I suppose, we try to understand what we must accomplish. Perhaps the most important thing of all is the attempt to understand others.

Understanding oneself—or at least making the endeavor—is tremendously important. Wise men have always known this. . . . I recently read something relative to the necessity of taking a little time apart, during every day, to face oneself without fraudulence. I have also heard it, within the past few weeks, from a pulpit. I'm afraid I'd not succeed, but as this is birthday month for me—and thousands of others—I do feel that a little stock-taking is in order. On my metaphorical shelves this past year—as in all years—I've piled up accumulations of goods. Some are dusty items that should have been used often—kindness for one, discretion for another, and trust; some are badly damaged goods, others faded, and many are items held over from other years. Also, there is equipment which I haven't sufficiently used, so it's rusty . . . for instance the tools which produce good will, spontaneous generosity, and praise. These do not operate by themselves, you have to take time, and trouble; you have to learn to use them.

There's bad equipment, too, such as the two-edged sword of sharp or careless words that can cut the person who uses it as well as the one on whom it's employed.

I guess I'll have to restock.

I wonder if anyone has ever looked back upon a year and found it, and themselves, perfect, the shelves stocked only with good things, continually in use, so, no dust gathering? I doubt it.

Now I have the months past to think about: the entertainment, amusements and holidays, the companionship of friends and the solitude of work. And I look from the big windows upon the silently falling leaves and upon those which tenaciously remain, and at all the color. For some years at this season I have gone out to look for brilliance and perfection in the leaves, detach specimens and send them south to the grandchildren who have never seen a northern autumn. They take them to school to show teachers and classmates, and then make a border decoration of them around their own windows.

This October I took more time. And collecting a number of specimens, taped them to a dozen sheets of paper and wrote upon each sheet the names of the trees: dogwood, burning bush, maple—protected each sheet with another, and sent them to the children in a big envelope, supported by thin cardboard as a further protection.

This is a good month in which to undertake new work, for it is mellow and mature, a bracing breathing space between too hot or too cold weather, and before the slow deepening darkness of short days. It's the month that

32

leads us quietly, almost imperceptibly toward the special official giving of thanks and the first idle snowflake.

For a little while my miniature zinnias will stay with me, and a few small asters. Tree leaves will turn brown and dry, but the flowers will blaze for a time, and every so often out of season a blossom will appear on a bush that should have been putting itself to bed. I assume that bushes and flowers do not consult calendars, they merely experience a moment of warmth, perhaps after a gentle rain, and so come perilously popping out.

This year the house has not been turned back to winter dress as it usually is right after Labor Day. The living room has for some time been imploring in a patient but desperate whisper, to provide new curtains, and then there's the matter of tattered rugs. I should have attended to all this last summer, but I didn't.

Throughout the year I write myself notes; most of which I lose, and if I find them, I can't read them. Now they'll be headed: What to do in October.

One thing I did on the first and second was to have two parties . . . one given me, another given to myself. And on the Cape in September, I had advance birthday gifts. One, Gladys Taber gave me; an enchanting driftwood panel with a suggested Cape landscape, which I can't describe; you'd have to see it for yourself. I brought it home, wrapped in a nightgown and sturdy brown paper, flat on the floor of the car. I reached the house in time to wash my face and stretch my muscles, and then go out to dinner. At eight that night the luggage remained unpacked and the mail unopened, while I snatched a row of books from a living-room bookshelf and set my panel therein. There was room for two books at one end, so I found the right ones—the wonderful book called *The*

33

House on Nauset Marsh, by Wyman Richardson, given me by my friend Eleanor many years ago; and the other, *The Clammer* by William John Hopkins. This once belonged to my mother and the date she has written in it is 1911.

Between the panel and the books, set a little forward, is an unusual oyster shell with a tiny fleck of orange on its humped back. It came from Wellfleet, from a private bed owned by the father of the host in whose charming house I ate it—or one like it. Best oysters, ever.

Eileen de Lory made the panel, which she calls "Nature Preserved." I think of it as marvelous impressions of the world about her.

I had many unusual and unexpected gifts this year. When I reached home on September thirtieth, Gussie was there before me, with armfuls of tiny mums, very branching, and hard to arrange even in the floor vases. I might add that this, too, I did after having dinner with a friend, and before unpacking. There was also a flower arrangement from my loyal friend Alma.

On the next day the flowers and plants came streaming over the threshold until I began to despair of unpacking, ever . . . and that night Nancy and Jean Webb—it's his birthday, too—took me to dinner. And on October second, a day late, I had my own party here.

Gussie had grown me a geranium tree and a coleus, and everyone was extraordinarily kind. A few more owls were added to my collection, including seven of them carved in, I think, bone, hung from a small necklace. It's American Indian work, a piece of so-called "pawn" jewelry, and was sent me by my younger daughter.

But presents and the innumerable cards, the wires and cables, are not just what they seem: They represent more than material things you can touch and see, taste, smell,

34

wear, or display. They represent thought, affection, and remembering.

In this month I'll be traveling by car to see my old friend, Mary Margaret McBride, in order to make a tape recording with her as I've done a couple of times in the past—a recording that will be used over the radio station near her. It's about a three-hour trip and great fun, and the road we take is beautiful. Once at Mary Margaret's, on the top of a small mountain, I'll look across the reservoir from the windows and the big porch—and dread to see how far the water level has fallen.

After that comes Halloween. Gussie will bring in fruit and candy and I shall have small change for those children who offer boxes to be filled for the less fortunate. In this neighborhood, those who come during the trick-or-treat hours are usually quite small, and their parents wait in cars, outside. The youngsters troop up the brick path and ring the door chimes. This is one evening on which I do not work, nor do I go upstairs until, at ten, I turn off the lights.

Some of my callers are choosey about the treats I offer them from the big kitchen bowl set on the table in the small entrance hall, but most are happy with whatever comes to their hands. There was a time when two of my girl grandchildren lived nearby and they, too, would appear hoping I'd not recognize them behind the fantastic masks; sometimes I didn't, which gratified them greatly.

Now in this month the birds have really decided to depart, but I'm sure at least a pair of mourning doves will stay, as well as the usual year-rounders. By next month I'll appreciate the blue jays. During spring and summer I speak chidingly to them because they chase away the smaller birds and, like starlings and grackles in their season, greedily consume most of the suet and seed set forth for any feathered lady or gentleman. But when it's cold and dark, when the snow falls, they are welcome to eat and run, as guests sometimes do, because I am grateful for their color, just as I'm grateful for the cardinals' kingly robes.

Now I look for pheasants and worry about the hunting season. I've seen them off and on all summer, and heard them in the distance. There's one male who has been here for years, I think. He grows steadily bigger and more beautiful, quarrels with the young males, and keeps an eye on the hens. I hear him speaking in the early morning and at dusk. He sounds rather like a rusty gate. And I'll be afraid for him next month, for, although my land is posted against hunting, I often wake to hear gunshots shortly after dawn. But perhaps game birds, unlike the bushes, have learned to read the almanac and know when the season of slaughter has arrived.

Also it's the time to put out the fat pumpkins—I already have tricolored corn at the door and in the Sung bowl in the hall. The big willow by the poor little pond is touched with pale gold, and the green holly berries are planning to turn crimson; the berries of the black alder and those of the dogwood are already red. In the fields, the grasses have faded to muted colors, beige and pink, and up on the Cape the bayberries are gray-blue pearls. The barberries, set in their thickets of thorns, are scarlet. I'd rather be in New England than in any other place at this season.

The other evening my younger son, his wife and two little boys came up from the city on their way to my older daughter's; they wanted to see the leaves. They spent the night here, and the younger boy, my youngest grandson Christopher, who was two years old last June, distinguished himself by a logical if somewhat terrifying re-

36

mark. He is at the run-and-shout stage, of course, and also in the imperious phase, pointing a small finger at anything, and declaring either "I want!" or "Mine!" Well, it takes a good many years to learn that what you want you cannot always have and that not everything is yours.

I had had my breakfast alone in the living room, for commotion is not my idea of the way to start a day. Later I went into the dining room fortified against almost anything. At which point, Christopher pointed his finger like a miniature pink gun, and announced that he wanted a piece of lump sugar. His mother said, "no," and added that it wasn't good for his teeth. Whereupon he fixed her with an outraged eye and said, loud and clear, "They're *my* teeth."

I am not usually given to repeating what's known as the bright sayings of children, but this one gave me pause. I shudder to think of subsequent years when Peggy may say, "Don't go near the edge of the roof," or "Don't climb that tree, Christopher; you might fall and break your leg," and he might reply, "It's *my* leg!"

Perhaps I have a little sympathy with him and his logic. How many times have people said to me, "You shouldn't live alone. Suppose you fall and it's hours before someone finds you. . . . Suppose you become ill." And I respond, "Well, that's the chance I take." In Christopher's reasoning, *my* chance.

Heavens to Betsy, I too "want" (and am not permitted to have, generally speaking), and I, too, look at something and think: Mine. But it isn't always.

I grow somewhat impatient with the much ado about the teenagers—I've some in my own family—and with all the solemn warnings and criticism, and with the phrase "in my day."

That day has gone forever, and a good many things

37

have gone into the making of this present day, which is also ours in the sense that we live in it. I deplore a great many things about today's youth, but their demands, their lack of discipline, of courtesy and consideration—these aren't the fault of the young but in most cases of their parents. As for the violence, perhaps that's the fault of the age itself, which is violent, and of rebellion, insecurity, and frustration. These have been part of the growing-up time of life, ever since there were families on earth. Only now, I suppose, it's easier to express such things.

In the hundreds of articles, books, and even sermons viewing with alarm our modern youth, I think the writers and speakers have forgotten that the troublemakers, the disturbers, and the destruction bringers do not constitute the majority.

Young men at this moment are fighting wars. And young men and women through the Peace Corps are waging peace, bringing education, help, and hope to many distant places. I know some of them. I also know younger people still at home, often critical of parental discipline but finding a certain security in the knowledge that their parents care enough to enforce it. I know boys and girls who, in difficult or average circumstances, are trying to adjust and to grow. I know those interested not only in study but in organizations through which they can bring something of value to others.

I suppose that all down the ages parents and outside observers have worried and often despaired of the younger generation. To be sure there have always been elements within it that do no credit to the society in which we live. But most adolescents turn out well—or well enough —and all of us who sit on the side lines and remark that things weren't like this when we were young are wrong; they were, perhaps with slight differences. And those of us who ask, "What is the world coming to?" must have heard our own parents ask it also.

What it is coming to, if we are fortunate, and also work to make it so, is something eventually better. And if that's a dream, well, I'll take a leaf from Christopher's so far unblotted book and answer, "Well, it's *my* dream!"

When Christopher grows notional, his older brother Stevie sometimes remarks, "He's just a baby." To which I might add, "Aren't we all?" For gray hair and the weight of years are not proof of maturity. And in many ways some of us are still just past two.

Now on the old trees the apples still glow, the oaks and maples stand tall and the road of the season leads through the cold flame of October to the ashes of November, the gray ashes which still contain a spark, an ember, the spark which is the spirit of the Thanksgiving month.

"To travel hopefully is a better thing than to arrive."

ROBERT LOUIS STEVENSON

I suppose that Robert Browning said much the same when he wrote, ". . . a man's reach should exceed his grasp . . ."

We are not always reconciled to this; along the road, we travel for the most part hopefully, always looking forward to arrival and we try, of course, both to reach and grasp.

I can't remember a time when I haven't, for ninety per cent of the way, hoped; the ten per cent given over

39

to despair and a sense of failure is as nothing beside the hope. As do many people, I have lived a good deal of my time in the inevitable daydreams—the "if only," the "perhaps" moods. I suppose I've never been a realist and, in a way, I'm glad. No matter how often in the twilight of dreaming or the soft blurring landscape of hope I've run into a stone wall, I've picked myself up and gone on my way, a little battered but still hopeful, and still dreaming.

The trouble is that most of us, old as well as young, experienced as well as just starting out, feel that things, once they are good, won't change. They do though; everything alters. But we tell ourselves, "This will last." We say, "This will never end." And when a situation, an environment, a way of life changes or ends, we are astonished.

The schoolboy cannot remain a schoolboy any more than the bride remains a bride. Success is a pleasant condition, especially if you feel that you have earned it and you usually believe, quite honestly, that it will go on. Often it does not and the adjustment to other ways of thinking or living, to different standards of success, is quite shattering at the time. But adjustment is possible, if not to the standards, then to whatever the alteration in one's personal life.

I have often said, as have a great many people before me, that when one door closes, another opens. This is, in the main true; although there have been times when I have looked in vain for the new door, it's always been there. I just haven't looked in the right direction, or I've been too egotistically blinded—or too stubborn—to recognize another door when I see it.

The road we now travel together has many turns and offers many obstacles. It also affords us magnificent views

40

when least we expect them, and little turnoff places where we may sit awhile and look back over the distance we have come, and toward the road ahead, although we can see only a little of it, for there's always the corner to be turned, always the unforeseen obstacle; always in a stretch of smooth going a patch of rough. There are hills to be climbed, there are plateaus and dark, wooded areas when we can't see the way before us. Everything can happen on the road: sunshine and storm, and the heavy enclosing fog that lifts to show us that the sunlight was there, just in back of it, even when we could not see it.

On this journey through a year or so, a traveler becomes footsore, grows tired, tells himself, "I can't go on." But he'll go on, because that is why we are here—to find the road, to traverse it, and to keep on going, which is in essence the simple secret of all success, of all adjustment, and eventually of achievement, which is more than success.

I've known a lot of alleged failures in my time and many of them, in losing what the world has always considered success, have achieved in facing up to failure, more than they ever achieved when they were considered successful.

Walking the path between what Helen Hunt Jackson called "October's bright blue weather" and Robert Burns's "chill November's surly blast" (why all poets dislike November I never have known), there are many things to contemplate along the way. As the days grow shorter and the nights seem longer and there's not much to entice us outdoors, work becomes easier and more personally rewarding, and books beckon to us from the shelves. As the squirrels have stored up nuts and acorns against the winter, we have hoarded memories of summertime and early sun and of the spring which seems

41

so far off, but which is merely just around another corner of the road.

I am creating my own time here, with a little pause between the months, where actually there is no pause at all as one day slides soundlessly into the next.

Upon this imaginary road, which may lead outdoors to actual roads, bordering actual places, or to roads that exist only in your mind or mine, or that may turn indoors and up a stairway I climb every day, or through a house I've never seen, let us travel hopefully. For, although R.L.S. did not say so, we will eventually arrive somewhere; that much is certain.

November

"And hold in the month of November
Thanksgiving unto the Lord . . ."

MARGARET JUNKIN PRESTON

The multicolored corn has hung by the door for some time. Each day I regard it, wondering how long the kernels will remain. One year, I recall, they were stripped in no time flat. So far they're not. Of course, only the front of each ear is bare when this happens. The birds can't figure out how to get at the back, short of a built-in drill, and I can't figure out how they even get at the front. There's nothing for them to perch upon except the light by the door and that's far above where we hang our harvest symbols.

Last year Gussie brought in especially pretty gourds; they looked good enough to eat—pale yellow, orange, green, and striped. Last year, I forgot to remove the gourds until Christmas and as I'd had them since, oh maybe September, they quietly crumbled to powder in my hands.

There's still color in the leaves, the muted kind I like,

but they came down early, I think because this year was so dry. Last year they lingered and there was water enough in the pond to sustain the mallards. I'd watch them fly by past the south window. This year I have none, and I miss them, particularly the pair which perhaps grew bored with the little pond and the fields and so came quacking up the brick path or across the grass, to sit on the rim of the millstone birdbath, and ponder.

I have no idea where, or with whom, I shall share this Thanksgiving. Perhaps I'll be alone, perhaps with a few people or many, but in any case I shall find time in the early morning, or in the twilight when I first see the evening star, to offer silent gratitude for many things.

All year I have been collecting small blessings as well as large, all of which I can think about and be thankful for. We are always grateful for the big things at the time they occur—and also later, when we stop to remember: for the unexpected rescue or solution to a problem, for the recoveries from illness of those we love; and for love itself. We also remember now and then to be grateful for food and bed, roof and health, friends and work. But the little benevolences, the small alms, so to speak, are often forgotten.

I am grateful for sleep, for the bright days in any season, and for laughter and sharing. I'm grateful for work accomplished, for the unanticipated friendly word or letter, and for remembrance of things past.

But, most of all, I think I am grateful for the small spiritual growth which enables me to accept the fact that certain gifts have not been bestowed no matter how much I've wanted them, and for that which has been taken away.

Acceptance is a far better word and denotes a more positive attitude than resignation; I've always known that,

44

but in recent days I've found one which is better still; it is consent.

I have been rereading several of my favorite novels, which recreate ancient Greece and other parts of the—to me—unknown world. Based on myth and legend, they come alive under the craftsmanship of the writers.

In two such books, both by Mary Renault, dealing with the old gods, the key word is "consenting": . . . a man goes "consenting" to his fate, and accepts it, wholly.

In this modern world there are also consenting people. I've known a number who in great, and constant pain, have consented to it. They accept and they endure and perhaps, in the acceptance, the pain itself appears somewhat lessened. This is not to say that they sink into an attitude of apathy, for most of them are fighters. They do not burden the people around them with complaints, they exhibit no self-pity, and they perform useful functions. They know how much physical strength they can expend without becoming worsened by it; and so, they expend that much, perhaps even a fraction more. They write, or they paint; they go to business, they see their friends. They undertake such household tasks as they can manage and while they consent to the conditions they are not in mental attitude or their spiritual outlook at all restricted.

It has been my privilege, over the years, to know many such people. One was my mother's mother, who lived consenting despite great infirmity, to be very old. Another was my friend, Eleanor. Still another, who left this particular plane of life last month, I had known for some thirty years, during most of which she was plagued by illness, which in no way kept her from doing, seeing, and going; and even in the last few years when she was more or less confined to her home, she was extraordinarily active in her mind, and alive and young in her interests.

There are also the people who, when grief or deep trouble comes upon them, go on, consenting.

One of my closest friends is always in pain. She goes on, she accepts, she conquers . . . and somehow the pain is borne.

When Saul received his revelation on the road to Damascus, he heard the voice saying to him, "It is hard for thee to kick against the pricks."

It is hard for us all; but when we consent, it becomes easier.

Long, long ago a man named Aaron Hill wrote:

> Tender-handed, stroke a nettle,
>   And it stings you for your pains;
> Grasp it like a man of mettle,
>   And it soft as silk remains.

I recall hearing this in childhood. I must admit I've never dared put it to the test, but I don't doubt that it is true. For the firm grasping of the challenge, whatever it may be, is a sort of consenting. You recognize the challenge, and you meet it, not by turning aside, not with a timid gesture and evasions, but by coming to grips with it, accepting it for what it is.

Now the skies darken early, and perhaps when I wake tomorrow there will be the first brief blowing snow or even a real storm. So I can be more grateful for spring and summer and the bonfires of autumn than I was when each of these seasons was all around me. For each is, in reality, so short we forget to give thanks and remember only to grumble when spring seems too brief, summer too hot or too dry, or any season, too rainy, and an early autumn, too suddenly, cold.

So I am grateful in November for the first violet I saw

in the spring, and the first tight dark buds of the lilac; for the long, sunny days and the cool, sweet nights, which often temper a heat wave; and for beaches upon which I have walked and the wide sea over which I have looked.

And for the first rose—my friend Agnes always brings me the first from her garden—and for the pansies Gussie picks in her yard and carries to me.

Almost a year has passed since last Thanksgiving Day was officially proclaimed, and in that year much has happened world around, in our own nation, and in the lives of each of us. However difficult, there has been much for which to be thankful. There's been a great deal to remember; and also to accept.

Soon it will again be Christmas. By Thanksgiving time we are all aware of this, and the tempo seems to quicken. Early next month I'll turn one of my mugs around. This is an old glass mug, heavy, and durable, and the color is a very pale yellowish-green. There's a worn gold painted line on the rim and an impressed pattern on the bottom. All spring it was filled with whatever small flowers I could find; violets, pansies, lilies of the valley, in the summer, with roses and wild flowers; in the autumn with little brightly colored leaves. But when I turn it around there is an inscription on it in red which reads "Merry Chrismas." Soon it will be time to permit the greeting to show and to fill the mug with sprays of holly from our own trees.

I am fond of the many mugs that are scattered all over the house, a number constantly in use for cigarettes or powder-puff cotton; some with dried arrangements in them, especially of sea lavender. Others I snatch from shelves upstairs and down to use for fresh flowers, as the mood suits me, the flowers, and the mug. Each of the mugs has interest and beauty, but the important thing is

47

that all have been given to me, so each reminds me of a friend. But this one, which is Christmas on one side and any season on the other, is special. For when it is filled with holly, I remember when it held violets or pansies or little roses; and whenever it contains a symbol of spring or summer, I recall that Christmas is just a hand's turn away.

Each season is a forerunner of the next, and as the earth revolves, we learn to adjust, and consent to, the alterations. It is not possible for man, with all his scientific progress, wholly to control nature any more than it is possible for him, for all his searching and philosophizing to understand God, Who being the Creator, has fashioned nature itself and hence the seasons in their orderly progression, whatever their occasional deviations from that which we term normal.

William Wordsworth, who lived in a less chaotic time than ours—although chaos is always present in one form or another in any era—wrote, "The world is too much with us . . ." And, in one sense, so it is, for he did not refer to the beauty and wonder of the earth.

But there's a remedy when we feel overwhelmed by the tempests in and out of nature, and by the world in its manifestations of violence, and hence, by fear and insecurity. It is in the Forty-sixth Psalm: "Be still, and know that I am God."

This is a month of stillness. Oh, I know the traffic still scurries, and the sound of guns speaking in the fields is frightening, and builders are hurrying to complete their clamorous tasks before winter comes. The windows still stay open, for we often have Indian summer during this month, even after the first killing frost has come. The true Indian summer appears warm and lazy, springlike and perilous. It's the time when people "catch cold."

Such a strange phrase; for when you "catch" something you do it deliberately.

Anyway, I still hear dogs barking and the hostile prowling of cats, hunting the careless bird. There's one cat I wish would decide to move to Florida; he lives too near me and my birds.

On five weekday mornings the school buses lumber by, and I hear children, laughing and calling. Nevertheless, it's a quiet month, a sort of holding-its-breath month, waiting for each turn in the weather.

Everyone should have a quiet interlude, spiritually speaking, and often. In the world—the one of which Mr. Wordsworth spoke—and in this age where there is always some noise and confusion; where there are sounds not only of construction but of destruction—and all the ceaseless sounds of progress, so called; when there are also the terrible sounds we hear in imagination—of wars and revolts, of weeping because of hunger, thirst, heat, and cold—arising from tired, dazed populations, a pause for silence within ourselves is more than ever necessary.

I sometimes think that people talk more than they used to, also louder and longer; including myself. Go somewhere—anywhere people are sitting or standing together, in homes, at parties, in restaurants, airports, railway or bus stations, even in shops, or out on the street wherever people walk—and it's impossible to shut yourself away from the din. Even in the theater or opera between acts, or sometimes during them. As for gatherings in homes, it's difficult to hear anything but fragments of conversation, if it can be called conversation. Everyone seems to be tuned to so high a pitch, and nowadays, it's a rare person who listens for long, to whatever anyone else says, when the group is merely social. (I wouldn't know much about directors' or other business meetings.)

49

It's important, if you can manage it, to take time out daily and shut yourself away for five minutes, or for ten. You don't have to go into a room and lock a door or hang outside it a sign reading "Silence." You can be doing anything—washing dishes, cooking supper, cleaning up the yard, dusting, or sweeping—and still remove yourself from uproar, even that of the vacuum cleaner. You can be with someone you love and by unspoken mutual consent experience a time of silent companionable peace. And even when you are with people all talking at once, you can withdraw briefly—they'll never know it.

When I am working—as now, for instance—I often take a moment out, no matter how close the deadline. A doctor who for years took care of me, a soft-spoken Kentuckian whom I loved, suggested long ago that I take a break every hour or so. "Go out and walk," he said. He also suggested that I do this before I began to work. I never obeyed him, I'm afraid. But I do, now and again, take my two fingers from the keys—for that's the idiotic way in which I type—and put my hands in my lap, after I have turned off the little motor that activates my typewriter. Sometimes I walk around the room; at others, I go into the living room and look from a window. But often I just sit still, not trying to formulate the next sentence.

The silence of nature is, of course, intensified by sound, which is not as contradictory an observation as it appears. When you walk alone in the woods, fallen twigs snap under your feet, leaves rustle, or bare branches creak and sigh in the wind. And in season birds sing, insects whirr, squirrels and rabbits scamper. It's the same in fields, empty of any human being save yourself . . . always, the little sounds that sharpen silence. Standing solitary on a beach, listening to the immense quiet of an ocean, or at the edge of a river, or beside a lake, there are sounds which serve to underline the essential basic silence: a wave crashes; a gull cries; a fish jumps.

Consider the golden silence of the sun doing its life-giving work; the silence of grass growing and of plants, seeds, bulbs, and trees rooting themselves in darkness and quiet for the winter ahead. Think of the mute-falling snow, of the moon before which clouds drift soundlessly, and of the silent stars.

In our inner selves the same pattern prevails; sounds reach us, but underneath there can be a space of silence.

At all seasons I am a devotee of the evening star. I don't really understand astronomy at all; but when dusk comes, I go often to the sun-porch casement windows and look for the evening star, silver, serene, hushed, and brightening as the darkness deepens.

When in this season rain comes or early snow, the rising wind often grows loud. Sometimes, of course, there is no wind, but when there is, there are sounds against the windowpanes. Wind-driven or not, raindrop and snowflake encounter the ground quietly.

Thanksgiving is very vocal: doorbells ringing, kitchen sounds, automobiles hurrying up driveways, and in cities hasty footsteps resounding on pavements. It is also full of the sounds of greeting, welcome, laughter, and reunion.

But it's quiet during the moments when we pause to offer the heart's gratitude, not only for the blessings of the months past but for the disciplines; and above all for the ability to believe in the future, whatever we may read or hear; to believe in friends, in love, in the world itself, no matter how troubled it may be.

These past months have been plagued by upheavals,

51

not only those caused by man himself—wars, fires, and the convulsions of earth eroded by the disappearance of trees—but by those disturbances originating in nature—floods, droughts, tornadoes, and hurricanes. I think of these natural manifestations as having been prepared in silence, and erupting into terrible sound—except drought, which has no voice—and, after the sound has ceased, falling back into quiet. And during these times of stress there is the courage of human beings, surmounting personal tragedies, the willingness to help, to clean up, and to rebuild. So Nature moves in her own and in God's mysterious ways; and man, in his.

Man has more courage than we give him credit for; and by man I mean all mankind, male and female, old and young. There are always the cowards, the evaders, the cruel and the greedy, but by and large the human being has great potentialities, and often fulfills them. I sometimes think the motto of the majority can be expressed in the words Queen Victoria once wrote to Lord Balfour: "We are not interested in the possibilities of defeat."

It's a good rule by which to live, shorn—dare we say? —of the touch of royal arrogance.

As to that, I have always been fond of The Good Gray Queen and have read many biographies, one very recently; I've also read letters written by her, for instance in the book *Dearest Child*. While I often disagree with her attitudes—or with her as she has been depicted, let's say—there are also times when I certainly agree. On the lighter side, how often I wish *I* could say with her crushing authority, "We are not amused."

I am frequently amused at myself (which I am sure Victoria Regina never was) as it is difficult for me to take myself seriously. Oh, there are aspects of myself I

52

do take seriously, such as my work, although I have no illusions about its importance, quite the contrary. I take seriously those aspects of me which make up attitudes toward my children and my friends and those which constitute (if that is the correct word) whatever philosophy I may have laboriously evolved; and also that aspect of me which in silence endeavors to find its way to the stars, be it day star or evening.

But the me that blunders about the house, types with two fingers, forgets what she had for dessert, and mislays everything from files to spectacles—I cannot take her seriously at all. In this case, if I may use the royal—editorial—pronoun, we *are* amused.

It is of some consolation to me that I rarely lose anything permanently. Occasionally, of course, I do—on the street, down a drain, or in a wastebasket—but for the most part I merely mislay. So things turn up again, even if in unexpected places; although when I find myself absent-mindedly looking for a wallet, a letter, or my glasses in the refrigerator, I'd faint if they did turn up there.

Very little, really, in life is lost; material things, now and then; money which is material but necessary, often; friends, relatives, sometimes through estrangements. True love never, I believe. Death does not rob us of the essential person we have loved and still love. It deprives us of the physical presence, but never of the spiritual closeness, or of memories.

There is one loss which is actually a reward, and that is the loss of oneself, in the sense of forgetting oneself, or totally mislaying it in empathy with other peoples' hurts and problems, in empathy with the whole world's difficulties, and even, for a short time, in the concentration of salutary work.

Now, while there is still a little daylight I think I'll go out and walk about on the leaf-covered grass or along the short driveway. It hasn't been possible to rake up all the leaves; it never is. But we try to keep them raked away from the house. The smell of leaves burning has been with us since last month. It hangs, of course, in ground mists and fogs, and we are told it isn't good for us, especially when cars and industries add to the discomfort of what is known as smog. But I love the burning-leaf smell. And while I, myself, do not enjoy creating any noise— if someone raises a voice, mine drops lower in protest— I like the sound I make walking in the leaves. As a child, I ran in them; now I'm content to walk and to feel the dry touch on my ankles.

This is a leaf-raking time, a time perhaps for house cleaning, as well as a quiet time. Most of us are tired when a day ends, and we think of the coming one as a number of hours into which we must put as much energy and work as possible. But, in every day, there are moments when we can pause, remember, think, be grateful, and add to our collector's items.

Memory can often be sharper than any knife, when a vanished day returns as an unbidden guest, to knock at the heart's door. But even painful memories are good because the qualities of being able to regret and to suffer in retrospect are given us for a purpose. I don't mean we should dwell on past trouble, old sorrow or mistakes, but it's healthy to remember, if, by remembering we can learn something.

I hope that this Thanksgiving, even if I forget whether dinner was a turkey or a beef roast, I won't forget to be grateful for the work accomplished, the night's rest, and the marvels of heaven and earth. For these we do forget, so often. And I sometimes think we forget

54

we are alive and breathing; we just go through the motions.

But because we breathe and are alive, and grow a little in order to expand the consciousness of all that lies within and without, for this we should also give thanks.

"There's night and day, brother, both sweet things . . ."

GEORGE BORROW

Most journeys are planned; we get out maps, book reservations, put the household we must leave behind us in reasonable order as we go off to pay a visit, take a holiday, keep business engagements, or see relatives. But there are unplanned absences, and they can begin at any time. Trains and planes often leave at odd hours; and people can leap into cars during any one of the twenty-four hours and travel rapidly toward joy or sorrow.

It sometimes appears to me that we journey through our individual lives almost as tourists, planning ahead, altering plans, or perhaps canceling them. We find ourselves in strange places and undreamed-of situations. We meet people we may never see again or some who become friends. And we are always looking about us, seeing, experiencing, thinking, hurrying, and often feeling, like the Psalmist, "a stranger in the earth."

Time as we know it is arbitrary, the hours divided into halves and quarters, into minutes and seconds. Yet actually we live in a sort of timelessness. Psychological time is not measured by clocks. The sixty minutes of an hour may seem a hundred times that, or an hour may pass, seemingly, in the time it takes to sigh.

55

Nature, however, has given us day and night. The sun rises and sets, darkness comes on quiet feet and the stars are shod with silver. The moon pursues her lambent course. Yet there are places in the world where nights are six months long, and so are days; places where there is no dusk or twilight, just bright day and sudden dark—and as Mr. Borrow's gypsy, Jasper, says, "both sweet things . . ."

We cannot always go along with Jasper's Romany philosophy, for us the day is not always sweet or the night. But pausing to look back, as over an old account book, I think the majority would have to concede that more were sweet than bitter. Almost every day has something to recommend it—a flash of hope, a moment of serenity, or a second of gratitude when a word is recalled which comforted or encouraged. In almost every day, however leaden the heart or feet, there comes a brief uplifting of the spirit.

And as Mr. Shakespeare said, except for the insomniacs and those in deep new trouble, sleep "knits up the ravell'd sleave of care."

I think of this artificial stopping place I've devised between November and December as a day and a night not to be found on any calendar or recorded by the tick of any clock—rather like a waiting room between trains.

So in imagination we can sit or walk about outdoors, however cold or threatening the weather, and we shall not feel the wind. Or we can remain within, in any room we fancy—one we know well, or one we've once known or one we've never entered except in books. I often find myself in rooms and corridors that were built by writers and exist only between book covers. There I can be with characters who inhabit a fictional or perhaps historical world.

56

There's always time to look back over the accounts which began from the moment we were conscious of ourselves as individuals. Sometimes we look back a long way; sometimes the entries are as close as yesterday. For instance, the Thanksgiving entry. How long a list we made just a few days ago of the people, circumstances, and things under the heading of "assets." Just ahead is the page for Christmas, another entry in the daybook ledger.

How do we approach the coming season? I wonder. And I answer myself, by reflecting: In a great many ways. Very often we approach it with fatigue, in anticipation or apprehension, with delight or remembered sorrow, and sometimes on our knees, sometimes walking, sometimes running, and sometimes with the lagging footsteps of reluctance.

I personally approach it with a mixture of emotions, and it is quite possible that only young children, those who have just become aware of the Christmas bounty, gaiety, and excitement, the Christmas carols and the Chrismas star—only they rush to meet the Evening and the Day with pure joy.

In whatever manner we approach, we cannot evade it. Many wish to. They fly around the world, they go on a cruise, or just shut themselves away. But they are met by Christmas; they will encounter it on a plane, a train or a ship; in a desert or on a southern sea. They cannot escape.

There's more to the quotation from George Borrow's *Lavengro:* . . . Sun, moon, and stars, brother, all sweet things; there's likewise a wind on the heath. Life is very sweet, brother; who would wish to die?

Christmas is sweet also. And high and holy days for those of other creeds; these, too, are sweet.

December

"Heap on more wood!—the wind is chill;
But let it whistle as it will,
We'll keep our Christmas merry still."

SIR WALTER SCOTT

Last year when I hung the sleigh bells by the door outside, I noticed that the short sturdy leather strap was cracking and the bells looked a trifle rusty. Goodness knows how old they are, I've had them for many years. . . . I wonder if, once, they were part of a harness and jingled as the horse-drawn sleigh ran smoothly over the snow? I can't even remember who gave them to me, or where they came from. But there they are still! And they have a right to rust in December weather; the strap still holds; and the bells still sound.

As in the last few seasons my big holly tree has been brilliant with berries, I cut the smaller twigs and branches to fill the Santa Claus vase, and the crystal goblet with the bright decorations glued on it and the stem encircled with little red and green and gold balls. So holly it's been for some years now all over the house. The tree has grown tall and wide in the more than a decade it's lived here, but not until recently did I cut any branches. When I do so, I'm careful, so that the shape is not distorted.

I must explain here that when I write my "almanac" books I kaleidoscope two years, maybe even three, but whatever the pattern, every year the decorations come down from the attic. A year ago last June, I think, my friend Alma, returning from a Cape Cod vacation, brought me three charming new angels, fashioned from little pine cones with bland, pink, painted faces and long yellow silken hair streaming down their pine-cone backs. No wings. They probably don't need wings; they've been too used to flying from a tall, tall tree of their own.

From Thanksgiving on, or even before, the Christmas spirit sweeps into the homes where the holiday is celebrated. It is silent and pervasive, something like a warm, rosy fog. "It lifts up the forehead," as Gladys Taber says. No matter how tired you grow with planning, shopping, and considering the always inadequate budget, the rose-colored feeling remains.

This season and the one which treads upon its heels always glitters with globes and tinsel; it is colorful with ribbons, fragrant with flowers and pine boughs, scarlet with holly and poinsettia, and melodic with singing and the chiming of many bells. Then, in a brief week's time we hear the blowing of horns. The Christmas and New Year's seasons are punctuated with parties and gaiety; but beneath bright wrappings and cheerful sounds are quiet joys, silent meditations, and moments of reflection upon the grave underlying meanings.

In this time of openhanded giving I think we should stop long enough to bestow on ourselves something very

59

valuable: the everlasting gifts of inner security, peace, and the trust which is so much more than hope. And we should greatly desire to give that security, peace, and trust to the entire troubled world. Sometimes I visualize a great living tree with wide branches that shelter the earth, and below the branches the gifts of love and peace wrapped in pure gold, tied with silver, and marked "For all the world."

How marvelous if this, our little earth, should wake one Christmas morning—or any morning for that matter —to find under this universal tree the gifts for which it has hungered and thirsted since men first knew hostility nurtured by fear or greed or love of conquest.

These longed-for gifts you cannot buy, nor can anyone manufacture them or put price tags on them. And no one person can give them to the world, although the desire to give must begin in individual hearts as prayer, then a joining together with other people also prayer-minded— and finally become prayer in action, through whatever service the individual can supply.

Prayer and service must be oriented by a passionate, necessarily impersonal, love for the world and all its people and the tremendous desire that all men be united in a spiritual brotherhood. Radiating from the single heart to the many, it can reach next door and across the way; it can peacefully invade every home in the community, the nation, and all nations. Each of us could be—if we thought about it and worked toward it—a tiny link in a great, jeweled chain, not symbolizing bondage but the flexibility of freedom. But not one of us is free as long as one man, however distant, unknown, or alien, remains enslaved by others, by circumstance, by hunger and poverty, or by his own thoughts.

So this is the gift I'd like to have a small share in giv-

60

ing: peace on earth. as the carols sing; love to the world; and freedom, the jeweled chain linking all men as brothers.

As the days draw on toward the shortest one in the year, we become more aware of the early falling darkness. Sometimes I go out in the morning or early afternoon, not to return until evening. If the sun is shining, if there's any light at all, when I leave I often forget to switch on the house and garage lights against my return at night. But when I became discouraged by the early descent of darkness and by my own forgetfulness, I remind myself that after the shortest day—which was, one year almost the longest I've ever lived through—the days begin imperceptibly to lengthen until, knee-deep in June, we reach the longest.

Now it is time for me to consult the almanacs—I have a stack of them going back for a long time—to see what the moon will be doing at Christmastime. Sometimes it's dark in this season, but not for long, and it doesn't really matter. Whether it shines as a silver sickle, half-grown, or in complete glory, the important thing is that it is there. We talk so much about harvest moons and hunter's moons, but rarely about the moons of Christmas, which often shine upon deep snow in this section, or upon just a scattering of white, or as this Christmas past, on bare black boughs. It's lovelier when the moonlight falls on branches furred in ermine. But we never know at the month's beginning what the days and nights will bring us. Ice, for instance. Sunlight upon ice, moonlight upon ice—this creates a magical glitter, almost too much for the eyes to bear, but also establishes peril for twig and branch and even big trees. I've heard them crack and fall —to say nothing of what can happen to the unwary walker

61

mincing across frozen roads or paths of brilliant patches of treachery.

My first Christmas in Connecticut was unseasonably warm. My children, enchanted with their gifts of sleds and skis, felt that they had been darkly cheated and therefore used a present which was meant for summer—an archery set. I also remember a Christmas when the weather was just bracing and lovely. We had early snow, which had melted on the roads, and now a clear warm sun and all of us went out for a drive. That night it began to snow silently, and on December twenty-sixth we woke with amazement to find thirty-three inches of the stuff in our back yard, drifts even higher, as the wind rose.

Every year I wonder about the little wild animals who live on this place and find shelter and sustenance, and about the birds we feed—some that stay with us all year, others that appear only for a short time. Except for the ceaselessly active squirrels, I do not often see the animals, many of which hibernate. Not long ago in the parking lot of my church I saw a squirrel, sitting calmly upon the spikes of a metal fence, quite unperturbed by his selection of a pointed resting place.

If it has snowed, I wake mornings to look from the window and to observe the signatures of the birds, for they leave their autographs—crisscross imprints, delicate and clear. If I wake early enough and raise the window shade, I often frighten the pheasants which have come to eat under the feeder. These are nervous birds. The least sound, or even a shadow, disturbs them and both the beautiful cock pheasant and the more sedately colored hen run wildly away.

Recently I thought about the red foxes I saw a couple of summers ago at my sister's place on Long Island. From the terrace I saw three of them, half-grown, playing in the blue dusk like carefree children, dancing and running, hiding and seeking, not making a sound. I called my sister and we watched them running around the bushes, jumping and chasing each other until the deepening darkness drained them of their beautiful color and all we could see were leaping shadows. I did not see them last summer. They were full grown by then, of course, and perhaps more wary. But I dare say they are still around, snug, this winter, in their secret dens.

Every year shortly after Thanksgiving, often before, I begin to collect gifts and put them away, hopeful that I'll remember where they are, but sometimes I forget, for after the chest in the library is brimful I have to take things upstairs and commandeer closet shelves and empty bureau drawers. Usually in October I start addressing Christmas cards, for those that go to my many friends Down Under in Australia and New Zealand, or Japan, the Philippines, and Africa must start their long journeys early. And early in December I start wrapping and mailing packages—if my stacked-away gifts turn up—and checking lists.

I always look forward to the tree trimming. For years now I've done it on December twenty-first (it's brought into the house the night before) and when I come downstairs on the twenty-fifth, there it is, and I'm as delighted and astonished as if I hadn't trimmed it myself, as if I hadn't been looking at the finished product for several days. Somehow it looks different on Christmas morning. Each year when I hang the ornaments, I name many of them for people I love who will not be with me here.

It is very difficult in the hurried, harried, often troubled lives we each lead to carry with us throughout the year the remembrance of a star dedicated to peace and the awareness of our personal responsibility, but in the last

63

few years I've hunted out the loveliest ornament of all to hang on a high branch under a star and name it for all the world. I have a number of metal stars of varying sizes, each with an inscription on it. These were given to me, a few at a time, by a friend in Pennsylvania. I've no idea where she obtained them, but they shine by lamp or sunlight. Under the big one which reads "Peace," I'll hang the ornament for the world, and wish peace on earth to all of us, peace in our personal pursuits, and in our hearts, and to each of us the certain knowledge that nothing we give freely and spontaneously of ourselves is ever wasted.

In the year in which I now write, no snow fell at Christmas, and we had the strangest melange of weather: too warm, far too cold, some rain—which we needed—and a great deal of sun so hot and bright that I found it impossible to lie down with a crossword puzzle or a book on the upstairs sun porch without letting down the woven shades, or even to sit on a love seat at right angles to the big south window downstairs. So while the world outside held its often very frosty breath, no snow fell. But soon it will.

Nothing new can be said about this season, nor, as far as that goes, about the heart's seasons of love or sorrow or trust or hope. It's all been said before, thousands of times and in almost as many ways. But if we can't say anything new, Christmas itself sometimes brings something new; perhaps a different melody for a familiar carol, an extra polish on the holly berries, an added sparkle to the tree within the house, and certainly a new wonder and a deeper hush to each receptive heart.

The Christmas season is so brief, and every year one hears complaints of fatigue and rush and hurry and too much activity, and even, "I'll be glad when it's all over."

But all this can be, and usually is, swept out, together with pine needles and bits of broken glitter, and when the Eve arrives and the tree stands fragrant and bright, and angels, however tattered, fly from doorways and stand on mantelpieces—I have a little one who always perches on my mother's clock—then in all but a few stubborn adult hearts the childlike expectancy stirs.

Year round in this old house, which is really beginning to fall apart here and there, there are some symbols of Christmas that are never banished to the attic but remain downstairs for very practical reasons. In my study I have a charming white cherub that feels not like porcelain, but bisque. It came to me years ago from California and at Christmas always appears in the living room; the rest of the time I can see it if I raise my eyes from my work. The pale green mug stays on the bookcase shelf; I simply turn it around. Upstairs I have a tall, beautifully colored plaster angel, who blows a silent trumpet. My younger daughter carried it in her hand all the way from Baltimore during a heavy snowstorm years ago. This angel is far too fragile to be sent to the attic.

I sometimes wonder why, living alone as I do and no longer having family parties, I bother to decorate the house and trim the tree. I often say, "I'll go away somewhere next Christmas." But I never do. I have been away at Christmas only once since I've lived in this state, and that was back in 1951 when I was with friends in the Adirondacks.

I see people, of course; family members come and go, and old friends, but if I never saw a soul, I'd still want the tree and the house ornaments!

Christmas, however, isn't a tree or holly wreaths, or music boxes and carols; it isn't shop windows, crowded with color, or the city or town streets festooned with

65

lights or massed with what are sometimes unfortunate decorations. It isn't greeting cards and cables, telegrams and telephone calls. These are all outward expressions. Christmas is rather a lift of the spirit, a warmth in the heart, a storehouse of memories of other seasons in other years, and of the people you love.

This year, Chanukah, the festival of lights, starts on December nineteenth, and in millions of homes the first candle will be lighted on that night and one on each night of the eight-day celebration. It is a beautiful thing to know that in so many homes, the world around, there will be Christmas-tree lights and Chanukah candles, all of them shining to the glory of God.

But whatever the season, we can light candles every day. I don't mean only in church or at home, but in our hearts, for there is no one season for gratitude and hope, or for the belief in a great and loving Power however difficult one's circumstances may be.

Christmas is for family and for friends; it's a time, too, when you hear from people with whom you haven't been in touch since holiday time last year. It is also a time to think of those who have no families and few friends, or who are living out their lives in institutions and hospital wards. I think that for these, the faceless, and the unknown, a candle should be lighted in the heart, as a wish that, no matter what their environment, some joy may reach them, some kindness, and that they may have memories that will not sadden but rather fortify.

Christmas means the open hand, offered not only to those close to us, but to strangers, nearby or a world away; an offering of empathy and help to the hurt, the homeless, the hungry, and the ill. Most of us live on —and often beyond—a material budget, but the budget of love can never be exhausted; as you give it, it is replenished; it is as wide and far-reaching as the seas; it is the blaze of a million candles and the reflection of God's love for all His creatures.

Being in a position to give, however small the gift, is a high privilege; an even higher one is being able to share. That is one of the profound meanings of this and every Christmas.

We pause on street or road to wish friends, acquaintances, and strangers, Merry Christmas. As the old song tells us, " 'Tis the season to be jolly." And it is so particularly for children, not yet old enough to have experienced disillusionment, and young enough to walk tiptoe for many days before the Christmas dawn. But I wish for everyone more than merriment and jollity. I wish them heart-warming surprises and loving-kindness; I wish them lights in the windows and on the trees and in the branching candlesticks; I wish them beauty and song and a gladsome coming-together. In short, I wish for all a blessed season.

And now I suppose I should tell you that past Christmas I did not have a tree. I came home from church on December twelfth feeling a little puny. The tree ornaments had been brought down in their big boxes to my study; and one single, very large box held the house decorations, and thank heaven was so marked, I think by Agnes, who has for years heard my plaintive asking, "Where is what?" I did not feel like reading or doing a crossword puzzle, or answering mail or working on a book that was facing a deadline. And I said to myself, rather petulantly, "I may as well decorate the house."

So I did. It took about two hours, and at the end of it I was tired, but quite happy with the result. On the next day I was to go out, so I called a taxi. But before it came, I decided to take my temperature. I did so. And then I canceled the taxi and my afternon appointment, crawled into bed, and telephoned the doctor.

The painful and frustrating effect of this sudden, and to me, inexplicable illness was that by the weekend I had said to Agnes, "Tell Charlie no tree this year," and she responded, "I hoped you'd say that!"

So, no tree, and the tree ornaments went right back up to the attic. I think they felt frustrated too. I was able to go out briefly on Christmas Eve, and to have here for dinner the friends with whom, for over a decade, I've celebrated Christmas Day. But I suppose I'll always think of 1965 as the treeless year.

There were trees outside, of course: the Faith tree (which wasn't named for me) is doing very well, thank you; so are the holly and all the others; and there was a little one which my daughter brought me for the terrace in a bucket of earth and trimmed with great slabs of suet. The birds loved it even though one wild, windy night it fell over and broke; but they stayed around it until the suet was gone.

So pain or no pain, frustration or no frustration, between my glimpses of family and friends and all the many kindnesses shown me, my treeless Christmas was also blessed.

"One of the pleasant things in the world is going a journey. . . ."

WILLIAM HAZLITT

I must, to those of you who are not acquainted with William Hazlitt, confess that the above is not all of the

68

quotation; it goes on to say, "but I like to go by myself."

Painter, philosopher, critic, essayist, William Hazlitt must have led a very full life and known a great many people; but apparently he liked to travel alone. Years later, Rudyard Kipling advised young men to do just that (but, for a different reason). Actually, I too enjoy solitary wanderings in the sense that I prefer to go when and where I please, without consulting or annoying a traveling companion by sitting up too late or rising too early, reading in bed, having meals at odd times and changing my mind about how I'll spend the day. Yet even on such selfish safaris you're not really alone all the time; you see friends, and you meet strangers. I can't tell you how many people I've encountered and talked with on ships, planes, trains, in hotel lobbies, waiting rooms, or over shared tables at meals. I'm still in touch with some of them, after years have gone by.

There was a time when, traveling, I delighted in the companionship of people I loved, but some are no longer here to go with me, and some are no longer able to. Therefore, as I grow older and doubtless more persnickety, I find comfort in independence.

However, in a small book such as this, if I am given one or two friendly readers, I feel that I am companioned. These unknown friends will not be disturbed by my peculiar habits, such as reaching airports, piers, or railroad stations hours ahead of time; insisting upon wide-flung windows in hotel rooms; breakfast in bed, if available; or by my insane aversion to sight-seeing. This stems from two things: First I've done a good deal of sight-seeing in my time, when I was traveling to obtain material and backgrounds for articles and novels; and second—and this one is highly contradictory—I don't like to sight-see alone or in groups. Alone, I doubt I'd cross a strange street to

69

see a spectacular monument or festival. But I do enjoy it when someone I know drags me out of a hotel, takes me about, and shows me what I should have gone to see in the first place. But the reader companion—if at all sympathetic—is not affronted by my habits and contrariness.

The journey between Christmas and the New Year is a brief one and, if we are wise, we will travel light that week. We will leave behind all the surface excitement and take with us only the memory and the meaning. And we'll travel without overweight luggage; we won't pack the old resentments; we won't burden ourselves with remorse and regret and will take with us only the best of the past. Henry Vaughan said:

> O how I long to travel back,
> And tread again that ancient track!

He was speaking of infancy and innocence. And most of us, I dare say, long at times to return to an earlier starting place, to have the road, new and shining, ahead of us. But when the longing becomes painful and the "traveling back" an obsession, we are putting lead in our shoes, and the advance, heavy-footed, into the future is a slow one. Wings on our feet would be better, though hard to come by.

There are some things we must take with us; the heaviest necessary luggage is that of responsibility, but anxieties and uncertainties weigh a good deal, too. We would not be human if we did not pack these into the valises. But there are things that weigh less and that we can carry forward into the new year: remembrance of love, of generosity, of blessings and rescue, of whatever small success has been achieved, and also the personal lessons.

These are not heavy as schoolbooks, but they're important. What we have learned this past year we can and should take with us; not that we always do.

A gentleman born around 42 B.C. once said, "An agreeable companion on a journey is as good as a carriage." His name was Publilius Syrus, and his translator, Darius Lyman, numbers this saying as Maxim 120.

I ran across him in a reference book. I have a passion for reference books. If I open a dictionary—I usually use the two-volume Oxford Abridged—to find out when a word first came into use, or likely as not, how to spell it and sometimes what it means, I am apt to spend an hour just dictionary reading. How remarkable are words and how baffling many of those in our own language. I am also addicted to encyclopedias of all kinds from the *Readers'* to my own battered set, purchased in 1928 and added to each year thereafter; and I love books of quotations. It was in one of the latter that I found Publilius. I haven't the remotest idea who he was; I haven't as yet looked him up (but I've no doubt that if ever a scholar should in a light-minded moment read this, he or she will write and tell me).

Anyway, Publilius had the right idea, although the notion of carriages in this century seems a little quaint. Come now as my companion—better than a carriage— travel with me into a new year.

71

January

"He giveth snow like wool: he scattereth the hoarfrost like ashes."

PSALMS. 147:16

It took me quite a while to establish this quotation as from Psalm 147. That's because I have such a hard time with Roman figures—as well as the ones we daily use— and in the Bible I have chapters were designated by Roman numerals.

If this past Christmas had been like the others, I would be mourning the banishment of my tree, which usually occurs just after New Year's Day, and I'd be removing the house ornaments. But they were put away early this year, and I've hidden the sleigh bells in the library chest. The red ribbons have been cut from the wreaths at the door, although the wreaths themselves will remain for a while.

Entering the new year is like going into a big and almost unfamiliar room. It can't be wholly unfamiliar, of course, as much of last year's furnishings are in it, but there are empty spaces and corners to fill, and new pictures to hang on the walls during the coming months.

Having tried to travel light, I hope I haven't brought the brittle, broken disappointments with me—they can cut like glass—or the faded shopworn things that should have been thrown out long since. I'm certain that every year in the new room articles turn up we shouldn't have brought with us, or didn't mean to bring—dusty, outgrown, awkward, and not suitable to the clean new spaces.

But some old things, the good ones, without which the new-year room would be very empty, are the qualities, emotions, and attachments we have cherished; these fit into the room like a hand in a glove. Love and loyalty—a quality rarer than one thinks—gratitude, remembered without embarrassment, and joy recalled, without mourning. No new room becomes one into which we can fit with ease and live with security if it lacks these.

I love color and light; yet in the heat of a summer day I want cool darkness. I love flowers all around me. So in this new room I'll have color and light to warm the heart and show the way; and when the heat of pressure is heavy upon me, I'll have closed shutters and a quiet moment for relaxation and contemplation. And I'll have flowers which can never fade: red roses, pink roses, yellow roses, sent me by people I have loved; a clutch of dandelions picked for me by a child; and the field daisies I do not forget. Tuberoses too. Many people dislike them because of their penetrating sweetness, but I have loved them for over forty years.

Over in a corner, on a little table, I'll put a Persian box and in it will be letters—hundreds of them, from many people. The originals have been destroyed long since, for I do not keep letters; but those which said memorable, or heartening, or splendid things I've noted to remember; they can live for twelve months in this room and in the one to follow.

I'll have a tape recorder, too—I've never owned a real one—and on the tape will be words spoken softly and with affection; words, bracing as a banner, which once gave me courage; and great philosophic sentences, which have remained in my mind since first they were read or spoken to me. Also on the tape, laughter and the easy talk between friends. These are recordings I can play as often as I wish during the new year, and I promise myself that there will not be one phrase of unkindness, or my own voice speaking in anger or impatience, despair or heartbreak. I shall not take such reminders from the recorder of my mind.

On the walls, new paintings . . . one of the little foxes of which I spoke last month; and my sister's Green Garden, now that it is established and growing; and portraits of new friends and of old. I'll have a still life too: a guest room overlooking fields and blue water and on a table little jars of tea, coffee, and sugar; a copper kettle ready to plug in, a silver tea ball, and cups, spoons, and saucers. I was in such a room last summer and woke shortly after six to brew myself some tea and read a book until my hostess and her husband stirred about downstairs.

Many of the pictures on the freshly painted walls will be old, having been part of my life for many years—the portraits, the landscapes of sea and sky and dunes; and here and there a small painting of a tropical beach or a southern lake; and of course Diamond Head, to welcome me back to Hawaii; and paintings of London—

74

small, secretive alleys and wide busy streets; a fine picture of St. Paul's Cathedral, and also one of a corner of Oxford.

It is easier said than done, this moving only the good memories into the new room, compelling oneself to discard the unhappy ones. But I find as the years go past and I move from one year's room into another, that I manage to take less with me of the things I do not need and should never have kept. I find, also, that I have more good solid comfortable furniture from last year and many more paintings, than ever before.

I forgot to mention books, and these are in my actual material house. There are fewer of them as I weed out or give away. But into this new-year room I'll take, from the many books which remain in my personal house, the few that, in coming months, I'll once more reread; and of course the things, also in my personal house, which, having been given me by friends, I treasure.

I hope to make the room of the new year quiet, which is not to say I'll be alone in it; friends will come and go, and my children and my grandchildren. But I would like it to be quiet in the sense that love is quiet, peace is mute, and hope is silent.

It should be a big room, so that the walls do not seem to close in on me; and the daylight should be steady and golden and the darkness rather like early dusk. There should be fresh air always, but not a troubling, restless wind. And the scent of remembered flowers.

Before the new year has run out I suppose the room will be cluttered with much that needn't have been put there, but, I hope, not as much as in other years. I remember times when the new-year room was so crowded I could hardly walk without stumbling over something carelessly dropped in a previous year and remaining as an obstacle.

75

January, in this section of the world, is a shut-in month for me and many like me. It can, of course, have its famous thaw and deceptive, almost mild, blue-gold days; it can also enclose us in snow, ice, and wind; it can bring blizzards. December has its imprisoning moments, too; and so do February and March. But somehow here we brace ourselves for January.

I shall be shut in, off and on, because of bad driving conditions. Not that I personally drive, but if I'm to go out, someone has to, and who am I to risk his or her neck, as well as my own?

So in this month I naturally think of shut-ins.

Many are, like me, shut in sporadically by the weather and the roads. Others are shut in most of the time because of crippling disabilities or long, serious illnesses. I know a good many; and still others whom I've not met write to me. These are people who are jailed by pain or physical incapacity or both.

I know some who are completely mobile physically, yet shut in by emotional disturbances; others who imprison themselves in real, or fancied, wrongs; and some who are encased within themselves by anxiety. These last I know well because I've often been one of them.

But it occurred to me the other day that no matter what the terms of the jail sentence—illness, pain, fear, worry—no one, however shut in, however immobile, or mobile, is shut *out*. None of us can be shut out from life unless we so will it. Whether lying for long years in bed, confined to a wheel chair with only infrequent outside excursions, or going about apparently free, yet through our own thinking, in prison, we are still inside life.

So we must look at what is around us, whatever our condition. Look through a window and see the world out-

76

side; it may not be a wide view, but it can be a deep one, and dimensional.

Books are windows into life, past, present, and future; friends are doors opening into the great spaces of love and understanding; one's family constitutes part of the wonderful world. Pictures—whether in books, on the walls, or on television—are also part of it.

No one—however preoccupied by pain, the incapacity to move about, or a handicap, however bound by the chains of worry and anxiety—is doomed to obey a sign which says "no exit"; no one is manacled to the point of no return.

I've known so-called hopelessly crippled people who, within the confines of four walls, have fashioned for themselves a marvelous, far-reaching freedom; through books, study, and patience; through love and a desire to go beyond those walls. Some have made careers. And I've also known people who, fettered by worry and personal distress, have broken their chains and reached out to others in unhappier conditions, and in so doing, have themselves escaped. To be shut in, by whatever seeming fate, is never to be shut out.

From my own many windows in this house I can look out on a January morning and see the snow silently falling and heaping up. I can hear the plows going through. I can reach for my telephone if the wires aren't down—usually they aren't—and call people to chat or break engagements. I can settle down to write letters or work or read. I can lie on a couch on the sun porch and watch the white, quiet world build up about me. I'm barred from road travel, to be sure, but not from the roads of imagination and meditation.

The winter storms will pass. The handicapping conditions of pain or immobility may never pass, but still the

77

world is around us in all its beauty and wonder. The active mind, even in an immobile body, may take full advantage of that world.

Now and then, when the snow abates and the howling wind dies down and there's no longer the shriek and rattle in my fireplace chimneys, I look out and see an intrepid bird. It may be a bluejay screaming defiance, or a pheasant mincing across the snow, or a chickadee swinging from a snow-furred branch, repeating his little song.

Small animals, during the night, write their messages upon the snow. They fend for themselves. They are never shut out; they venture into the wintry wilderness to seek sustenance.

No matter how shut in we are by weather, by physical handicaps or by such mental conditions as we manufacture for ourselves, we are still free people as long as the mind functions, the imagination is stirred and the desire to reach out, to experience, feel and know, is with us; as long as the heart beats and with it the pulses of love, interest, and empathy for and with other people.

"No man," said Donne, "is an island, entire of itself." We may think we are alone. We are not. No one is, not ever; not in ocean wastes of anxiety, the desert of grief, the depths of pain, or the dreadful uncertainty of *thinking* we are alone.

None is, in the deepest sense, nor ever has been.

I'm writing this in mid-January and despite all my weather reminders, we haven't had snow yet this year. Once, after dire warnings, we had just a gentle scatter, which by next day, midmorning, had disappeared. Bitter cold, yes—and so much wind. Gorgeous sunsets, red dawns, but no snow. Now I'm told it will arrive tomorrow with trumpets blaring. We shall see. It's been all around us: in Boston up north and in the snow-belt cities. We cannot deceive ourselves; it will come and plenty of it, but just now I'm grateful that it hasn't.

I had to go away recently, once to Long Island, once to Jersey City, both long drives and while it teemed rain one day, it did nothing worse. And however freezing the weather during the transit strike, at least the poor people, New Yorkers and commuters alike, walking to work, if possible, did not have to struggle through drifts.

Just after Christmas a dear friend, talking with other friends, happy and gay, was taken suddenly ill and not many days thereafter went away from us without regaining consciousness. At her services a week ago, a blowing, icy, sleety day, I sat next to someone I'd met at my friend's house and who'd known her longer than I. She said, "We are all poorer. . . . In all the time I knew her I never once heard her say anything unkind about anyone."

I do not think that there could be a lovelier tribute for anyone. Our mutual friend was right, and certainly we are all diminished.

Yesterday (and the day before) it was like early spring, cool as an ice-cream soda, but the wind had dropped and the sun was golden bright. I was working, but Gussie called me to announce that I shouldn't stay in. So I didn't. She came for me around two in her little car and we went rollicking about side roads and main ones for over two hours. I looked with astonishment on places, nearby, in my own town, that I'd never seen: vast developments, houses, apartments, office structures. I couldn't believe it.

Gussie has a passion for looking, as a passer-by, at new houses. We don't often agree on them, but it was a great deal of fun and while it didn't advance by an inch the work I had to do, or put off the dreaded deadline, I think it did me good. Fresh air, warm sun, and many surprises.

Now, I believe the gloomy-weather boys are correct; it's only a little after four and the sky is beginning to wear a heavy gray cloak. Only yesterday I thought that the days had really begun to lengthen!

Janus, the two-faced: one face of gold and one of pewter; one face that smiles with a certain cheerful kindliness and another one that frowns and threatens.

I have a stock of new books from the lending library. I think I'll make a phone call or two, write some letters, then choose a book, either old or new, and go up on the sun porch to read. As this is a day on which no one else is in the house, I can come down early to get myself some supper or later just as I please.

It was, of course, Shelley who said, "If Winter comes, can Spring be far behind?" Yesterday I believed him, tomorrow I probably won't. I'll say, "It certainly can!"

The ground is frozen now, perhaps not yet deep down; the birdbath has been frozen for weeks but occasionally melts around the edges and the birds can have a small sip. I wish I could supply them with straws. Yesterday, during our ride-about I saw children skating for the first time this year. On ponds maintained by towns the soft, edging spots were barricaded off, but on others, there were no barricades and I worried lest some youngster, skating freely, should fail to stop in time. Gussie remarked that maybe the pond I was contemplating wasn't deep. Well, maybe not, but it would be certainly cold even at the edges.

Two-faced Janus or not, I insist upon thinking about spring; and all the secret growth beneath the hard ground, the green things sleeping and dreaming and pres-

80

ently, even though we do not know it, they will be stirring.

Isn't next month the month of the ground hog and his shadow? Let's hope he doesn't see it, though logic reminds us that he may see it in one place, and retreat to his further slumbers, while twenty miles away the sky may be dark and he won't see it at all.

Now that January is half over, we head toward hearts and flowers anyway.

Happy Year of the Horse. Our Chinese American communities celebrate it with dragons and firecrackers on the twenty-first . . . and in Vietnam there'll be an uneasy lull to usher in the year 4664.

"Now spurs the lated traveller apace

To gain the timely inn."

SHAKESPEARE

It occurred to me in the middle of last night that we have been traveling together for five months, and I've never even suggested a picnic. This was a terrible oversight. In books of autobiography, biography, travel (in all countries), and even in fiction, writers concern themselves a great deal with food and drink. In travel books it is very important.

Personally I think I should have packed a lunch or prepared a picnic for each month although, in the cold ones, the choice of what should go into a hamper would be difficult.

About places and food I've always had romantic ideas, mostly derived from books. I was once in Rome for a

81

few hours—we were supposed to be there a shorter time, on the long flight from Sydney to London, but our plane became somewhat temperamental, so for those of us who desired it, the airplane line arranged a bus tour of the Eternal City. I went with some English people I'd met when they got on the plane at Bangkok. Each of us was provided with a box lunch. As the bus careened around curves and the guide, clinging to a metal support in the middle of it, recited the city's glories past and present, I dreamed of fresh fruit, marvelous cheese, good bread, and a little mellow red wine. What was my astonishment to find within my box a sandwich of something which looked like field rations, a pickle or two, plus a miniature carafe raffia-wrapped. I was forced to pull the cork with my teeth (which haven't been the same since) and as there was no other fluid around, I took a cautious sip. A more acid brew I have never encountered and I fell into a coughing fit which amused my English friends, sitting in back of me. They leaned forward to smite me on the back.

However, my traveling companions in this book and I have a choice of picnics, box lunches, or a restful meal at some imaginary or remembered wayside inn.

My friends know I can't cook. I know it. Now you know it. My friends are also aware that I like strange as well as familiar food, but not much of it. Left to myself, even though given the widest selection possible, I'd probably die happy of malnutrition. How long could I live on fresh Beluga caviar, a delicacy sent me annually by one of my agents? It comes in what looks like a cold-cream jar, and I'm apt to hide it in the refrigerator and offer it to very few people. And I shall probably never again taste the tiny, wonderful Australian oysters, but I'm reasonably sure of lobster on the Cape, boiled, hot and sitting up on a platter with its claws folded, heedless of its doom.

Once upon a time I told my father I had never had as many marrons as I'd like, so he produced them for me one night after the theater, a whole dishful. It was years before I could look a marron in the face again.

Now and then I find myself munching through mountains of popovers or their related Yorkshire pudding. And when I visit my sister, she buys blowfish—you use only a small part of it—and I recall that once while she was preparing them for our supper, all the lights went out. But she managed and we groped our way through this delectable dish.

Oh well, I'm fond of all sea food except the clam which has a tendency to poison me.

One way for us to eat, each with personal preference, discrimination, and pleasure on this trip and yet never have indigestion, is to read cookbooks.

I do. I've never had the least desire to put the recipes to the test but now and then someone writes a cookbook with a running commentary, spiced with humor, and gentle with reminiscence. These I read the way you'd read a novel.

One such is Gladys Taber's *Stillmeadow Cookbook*. I can read that, think myself back to Stillmeadow itself, the old old house in the woods, the hills and meadows, and the Cape, and relive our years of friendship.

My favorite supper dish is in the book. How often have I asked her: "Isn't it time for the fried tomatoes, bacon, and cream gravy?" So she prepares it for me. I am hurt to the quick that the recipe is not entitled "Faithie's Favorite."

Well, you may break this journey with whatever energy-restoring picnic or dinner you wish, and with no regard

83

for what I might at the moment desire. I am, anyway, a very indecisive character. When I go out with people to a restaurant, I wait until I hear what they order before I do. Or having ordered from the menu, I look at those at the next table and wish I'd ordered what they have. When guests are expected in this house and Gussie inquires, "What shall we give them?", I am as horrified as if confronted with a problem in calculus. When I'm alone, she serves what she thinks best, and I gratefully consume it.

But on our travels, you may have whatever your taste demands, to sustain you from chapter to chapter, and if I decide on fried tomatoes, Beluga caviar, and Australian oysters, you'll never know it!

Have you ever read the letters of Sir Richard Steele to his wife, Prue, which were selected and collated in 1927 by R. Brimley Johnson? These are delightful communications written in a time when the only communication was by post. They are delightful and sometimes surprisingly modern. In 1707 he wrote his Prue, enclosing two guineas and added, "Dear Prue, I can't come home to dinner."

Imagine someone in a twentieth-century business office doing that . . . and thus being spared the matrimonial wail he would have heard over the telephone.

Probably one of the most modern things Sir Richard wrote was the brief sentence: "I am busy about the main chance."

Aren't we all?

Now it is time to close the door on January and open the one, decorated with hearts and flowers, which leads into February. Bring an apple with you, a sandwich or a pot of tea—I'll ask my sister to lend you one of her quilted cozies.

84

February

"Well dost thou, Love, thy solemn Feast to hold
In vestal February."

COVENTRY PATMORE

In another poem, Mr. Patmore tells us that "of all the seasons" he "most loves winter."

I cannot go along with him there, unless it be winter in a southern climate, although I must recognize the peculiar loveliness which can, in February, in New England, lie all about us. As for the hearts and flowers I mentioned a page or two back, do not wear them, one on your sleeve, the other as a corsage. They'd freeze.

This is a difficult month, but it has its compensations. It's short, for one; and it's nearer spring than is January. Sometimes we have a thaw as well as storms, steady falling snow, or just plain dreaded blizzards, when I scream, "Has anyone checked the generator?" (Of course they

85

have: Charlie, who does so weekly, never fails me.) But now and then when I've been house fast for a time and finally wake to a day all sparkle and pale blue sky and look out on carven drifts and laden trees, I think of Ralph Waldo Emerson's delightful phrase, "the frolic architecture of the snow."

Next Christmas, Heaven willing, I'll have my Florida grandchildren with me for a visit. They yearn for a white Christmas—they would have been heartbroken had they been here this Christmas past—but I shudder to think of snow in their galoshes, wet socks and mittens, and of the windy chill to which their thin-blooded innocence must be exposed. And I suppose I'd better start saving now for bundle-up clothing and sleds!

Cardinals have been with me thus far, mourning doves, and the amiable cheerful birds who are year-round residents. Going out to the feeder is a cold process. Sometimes Agnes does it for me and then I watch the blue jays scream their way down to the bread bits we offer. On Saturdays seed is put in the feeder; by Monday it's gone.

This is a good month in which to ponder on love—any month is, of course—but when I write, address, or open valentines, I find myself moved beyond the familiar meaning of the date. I like to send valentines. People expect Christmas and Easter cards, but—once past a certain age—many don't expect valentines.

Love isn't all roses and moonlight, flower arrangements and boxes of candy, or even Cupid with his sharp little weapon. Love, in other words, isn't just for lovers.

It's for everyone, relatives, friends, strangers; it's for all humanity.

Early this month I look for enormous valentines to send to the youngsters in the mountain schools I sponsor,

86

one for each schoolroom to be tacked up, I hope, on a bulletin board.

Nowadays it's routine to say, "Live a little." Well, no one lives a little, no matter what his circumstance. He lives a great deal every day and minute, whether he knows it or not. And saying, "Love a little" doesn't make sense either.

The capacity for loving varies with every human being; some love the people and the world around them as naturally and spontaneously as they breathe. Others do not. Love is often wrung from them almost reluctantly, and it's hard for them to expand it much beyond their own small circle.

But expansion and understanding come, I dare say, with learning to use one's capacity and thus extend it, in both the personal and impersonal ways of love.

I look from winter-frosted windows and love the white world no matter how trying I find it when I venture out. I love it for its singular beauty and silence and for what it reveals of Nature.

When I go out, however, I complain loudly and snatch at any straw—even a broom, wishing I were a witch —to keep myself upright on the brick path, and I shudder when a car I am in decides to skid toward another car or a stone wall. Stone walls look soft under their blankets of snow, but they are not.

It's the same with loving people; we complain about them, we are hurt by them, we misunderstand and are often made unhappy by them, yet that need not affect loving them any more than the discomfort and sometimes danger of a winter day need affect one's appreciation of its beauty.

It's easy to love a dazzling summer day—if it isn't too hot, or humid, but clear as spring water. It's easy to love

87

a person who is lovable in the best sense: kind and gay, compassionate and outgoing, friendly and good like my friend who left us last month.

Ah, but the wintry people, those who sometimes appear frozen, those who moan like a north wind in the chimney, those against whose façades you can bruise yourself, and those with perhaps slippery spots in their natures—that's not as easy, but it can be accomplished if we work at it, for a winter aspect often hides the warmth of spring.

In this month, I usually think of the South and plan to journey there. It doesn't always come to pass, or maybe the dates must be altered. Sometimes I fly off looking down on a snowbound world and knowing that I'll step off the plane into one that is green; and often, returning from the green world, I re-enter the white one.

So I'll sit out February, dreading, in my cowardly fashion, icy roads and banked snow and sharp disgruntled winds, which seek out every chink in your woolen or furry armor. And I'll wait to see if it is feasible to head for Florida, though my objective in going there is not really to escape three weeks of New England winter but to see people I love. So when someone wishes me a "happy landing," it doesn't mean just safety and sunshine.

Anyway, I'll wait and see. Each day will be a fraction longer, and if anything can make the seemingly paralyzed hands of my clocks speed up, it will be work. For winter is a good time in which to work; there are few temptations to cover the typewriter and run outdoors.

Sometimes in winter the sun is so pale that you can look directly at it, and with the brilliance of stars on an otherwise dark night there comes to the contemplative heart the sense of the earth turning, of seasons following a rhythm, and the awareness of Nature, immensely busy and adhering to the pattern the Creator has ordained.

It's all so orderly. Even months when the last dead leaves rustle past, untidy as they seem, they have order. It's the fashion today to believe we live in a world without any order, one which is for the most part chaos, violence, and uncertainty. But that's not true. Men make the chaos, attract the uncertainty, and choose the violence. This is not in the original, basic pattern. Only man, in his blindness and folly, for all his progress in many fields, distorts the pattern, wrenches it out of line, and shape and order. But at the core, the pattern remains untouched.

Look at the stars one of these nights. Think about them and the charted courses they follow. Think of the sea, if you are close enough to observe it; or of a river; meditate upon tides and their rise and fall, upon storms and the quelling of storms. I once saw on television a documentary that traced the Nile from its small beginnings for four thousand miles to its final goal. That's order.

Sometimes it seems almost impossible to bring into our own small personal lives any order whatsoever. We may think for a short time that we have succeeded and then, with or without warning, the confusion starts again. But this too is a type of ordered activity—physical, emotional, or spiritual, as the case may be. From the disorder we ourselves create we are supposed to bring about order once again and in the process to have learned a lesson. I don't say that we always appreciate the lesson, but it's there.

When man in his greed cuts down trees, destroys beauty, and then finds himself with a land eroded, a dust bowl or a place of infinite ugliness, he must eventually repair his mistakes; he will plant trees, which will take a long time to grow; he will seek scientific help; he will try to

89

re-create something of beauty. That's learning a lesson the hard way.

Once, driving through the land of my host, I saw how prosperous an enormous sheep station was; how clumps of trees had been left standing and fields held back, so to speak, against a famine, and only a few sheep run, as they say, to the acre. His neighbor's land was almost ruined by the removal of trees and the lack of foresight; so his sheep starved. One man created chaos out of order; the other preserved order, his acreage, and his animals. I've always remember this, although I saw it many years ago.

Order is one of the first principles. There are others. Balance is a part of order; so are justice, love, and light.

This small world of ours, the sun, the moon, the many stars are all very old, and earth has passed through eons of change and alteration. But always the creative plan remains.

Now, in the snows of February, I can see the steady progression toward the spring, and while I am often dismayed by sudden storms—just as I am by the hurricane season or times of drought—I take heart. For order will be restored.

I suppose that's the way to think of our own lives, so often disrupted, uprooted, torn by a grief or fear, as by great winds, dry as a desert in the times of doubt. I believe we should think not only "this too will pass," but "order will be restored."

Each heart has its own private seasons, and the mind and spirit also. No man lives perpetually upon the peak of anything, whether it be grief or joy or fear. There are mountains to climb and wastelands to cross, but there are also plateaus.

Someone wrote me recently, "You always seem so optimistic." Oh, but I'm not, in the usual sense. Hopeful, I think, is the better word.

Now before the snow falls again, I'll put on boots, go out and look at the birdbath; the water's frozen solid. I can't use the hose, of course, but we do try to take out buckets of water (even if it freezes as we carry it). I've even tried hot water. And there are signs that bird claws have skittered over the ice. But the birds are not despairing; for given a little period of February sun the ice will melt long enough for a drink, if not for a bath.

The route to the birdbath is often mountainous with snow; sometimes it's frozen and affords a crusty sliding surface. I've always been afraid of falling, especially of falling downstairs. This causes me to descend rather like a timid crab. I once asked my mother if I'd ever pitched headlong down steps, having by then heard of traumatic experiences, and she said firmly, "Certainly not!"

I then came to the conclusion that in some former reincarnation someone had chucked me downstairs, and maybe I'd deserved it. I've said and written this often enough for people to cluck at me, and cry, "What a silly notion!"

Maybe it is but I was as scared of falling downstairs at ten as I am at more than three score and ten.

I've also always been afraid of falling on ice, or even in snow. I remember before my first child was born we had an icy, snowy March and, bidden exercise, I tottered along city streets, clinging to any kindly offered arm. I did fall—once, but as it was in a gutter heaped with snow, I wasn't hurt, except for my pride.

Sometimes after I've spoken to a group, a few hardy listeners will come up to me and remark that it's so nice that I have a sense of humor, and I am constrained

91

to reply, "If I didn't have, I doubt I would have survived to speak to you here today."

A sense of humor is an odd thing, it differs a little from a sense of fun and wholly from a passion for practical jokes. It's mostly, I think, a sense of proportion, of knowing, or at least thinking you know, what's important and what is not. Learning to laugh at yourself—and that takes time—isn't a sense of humor as much as it's balancing of scales. Sometimes in speaking to would-be, or beginner, writers, I try to impress upon them that they should take their work seriously—whether it's good, bad or indifferent—but never, never themselves.

Someone just came in and picked up the untidy crossed-out written-over and generally dreadful sheets of paper so far achieved on this chapter and remarked loftily, "I thought you were writing about Valentine's Day and February."

Oh, very well. Can I help it if I digress? I was born with a grasshopper mind.

Now in February I look back over time elapsed; the happiness of Christmas, the promise of the New Year; and I also look ahead to spring and to the summer, which must follow. The ability to look back and also to look ahead is something we've all been given. We know that the past has gone, except in memory, and that the future is veiled. We know that today—this hour, this moment—is all we can say we possess. Yet we are able to look back often with regret, but always with wonder, and to look ahead usually with hope.

Each year, month, week, and day is an unopened gift when it arrives. We do not know what it may hold, but as we grow a little older and wiser, if we remain young in heart and spirit, we can open each package with trust and with fortitude.

92

So I'll think of my valentines, whether they be eight or eighty, love being with us always.

"Take flight and follow and find the sun."

SWINBURNE

All right, so that's cheating a little. Mr. Swinburne was not writing about airplanes in this celebrated poem. Actually he was speaking of swallows (and I judge symbolically), but I have taken one line out of context and read into it my own meaning, which is, follow the spring and discover the sun.

I often think of my first flight, which took place from a Naval Air Station back in 1920 and was not only against regulations but was a sort of daring adventure. And of subsequent air travel, rare at that time and on my part reluctant. Now I bounce on and off aircraft beset only with minor anxieties: Am I sure I have my tickets? How much overweight is my luggage? Can I be sure of a window seat? Things like that. I'm certain that birds have no such worries and if there's a storm, they can hide in the woods.

Traveling in a jet you do not see the earth once you are twenty or thirty thousand feet above it. One of my little grandsons on his return flight from the North to the South informed the passengers that they were now traveling in outer space. Well, it's outer enough for me.

Taking off and approaching a landing you are, of course, aware of highways so small they could fit in a pocket, houses built for dolls, swimming pools like drops of water and cars you could hide in the toe of a Christ-

93

mas stocking. But high above these you have the clouds. Once, during the First World War, I was in a car with a young English flier, who looked at the great fleecy clouds over Montauk Point and told me smugly, "I know what those look like from the other side."

So do I now. I also know what it's like to be winging along under a full moon and a starry sky and look down to see banks of fog.

On one such occasion, flying home from Florida with my young Janet, we were informed that, weather conditions having worsened, the plane couldn't land at Washington or Philadelphia or New York or Boston. I was rather new to flying in those days and when a passenger-started rumor reached us that we'd have to land in Providence, I sent Janet into a fit of the giggles by saying dismally, "But I don't *know* anyone in Providence!"

Anyway it was hard to believe that airports were closed to us, for if we didn't look down, all we saw was the clarity of the moonlight and the sequined sky.

Maybe, when our personal fog closes in, it's well to look up.

There was a time when I did a good deal of cross-country traveling by train. I always loved it and was conditioned to it from childhood. I liked the little comfortable rooms in which I worked or sat or slept; I liked the dining cars and the lounges and the ten- or twenty-minute stops. I'd get out and walk on platforms in strange places, careful not to go far from my car, as I was always convinced it would depart without me. Hardier souls would rush into the depot or even stroll out on unfamiliar streets, but not me.

Once, going to Hollywood to talk to a motion-picture producer, I was enchanted by being paged at various stops and handed extravagant telegrams. It made me feel

94

ten feet tall. On the way back, I had just two, however, one from the producer, wishing me a good trip, the other from the Western Union girl in my hotel. She missed me, because I had no sooner reached Hollywood than I too had fallen into the habit of sending to my family long, detailed, and sometimes insane wires. After a week I was wiring: "They have given me two dollars and a new suit and I'm on my way home."

All the trips were good and I especially liked to look from the compartment windows at night and see the lights spring up in big houses and small. Once I saw—and have often written of it because it was magical—a meadow, and standing in the meadow, a cow. Now this is hardly breath-taking; I've seen lots of cows and meadows in my time. But this cow was standing in a rainbow. How this happened I don't know, but there she was, placidly munching away with her back and flanks striped in the rainbow colors. I have often wondered if she was really looking for the pot of gold. Anyway she was far more spectacular than Gelett Burgess' famous Purple Cow because she was all colors.

I've twice seen rainbows which were to say the least rather rare; once tinting that cow and once from the sea, over black lava in Hawaii.

Glimpses of houses at dusk, or at night from a moving train set the onlooker to wondering what sort of people live in the little house or the big one—a family, a solitary householder, a young couple who have just moved in. Are they happy? Are they well? What does life hold for them? What has it held, for old and young?

In a city you don't see as much of other people's lights from your own apartment or hotel room, and somehow a lighted window across a courtyard does not hold for me much magic or even speculation. But once I did see a couple quarreling—no, twice—different couples. But here in the country if I happen to get up at dawn or shortly after, I can see the neighbor's lights go on, and so get to know who goes to work early or has to commute by car or train. When, however, a light goes on suddenly and it's still dark outside, I always wonder if someone is ill.

Life is rather like a long train ride; you may encounter a great many people, but looking out from your own small compartment of self you catch only a glimpse of other people's joy or despair.

The sound of a jet taking off is special; the sound of a train whistle in the night is, too. It is not as melancholy when you yourself are on the train, I think, as when you hear it from your house as I sometimes do.

William Ellery Channing, who died at the turn of the century and therefore never saw a jet, wrote a poem called "The Earth," and beginning "My highway is unfeatured air . . ."

So, if you are willing, suppose we fly together into March.

March

*"Tossing his mane of snows in wildest eddies
and tangles,
Lion-like March cometh in, hoarse, with tem-
pestuous breath."*

WILLIAM DEAN HOWELLS

That's from a poem called "Earliest Spring" and as Mr.
Howells lived in Boston, his conception of March as a
lion would usually be accurate. But sometimes the lion
turns lamb.

This year I shall not be going to visit the older of my
two Janets, whom I've known since I was fourteen; I'll
miss her and her beautiful house, the lagoon and the
Gulf, and all the friends I've met through her on Siesta
Key during the past five years. Instead I'll head for Janet,
the younger, and take up my residence in the hotel where
I've stayed for the past five years after my Siesta visit was
over. I'll find old friends there in Winter Park. I'll walk

and shop and invade bookshops and, late afternoons and weekends, I'll be with the younger Janet and the children . . . that is unless something intervenes.

Some time ago friends invited me to spend six months in Mexico. I could no more spend six months in Mexico than in Tibet, but it was pleasant to know that they wanted me and I wished so much to see them—and incidentally I love Mexican food, the hotter the better—but to that invitation I was forced to reply firmly, "Thank you, but no." Usually I say "Perhaps" or "We'll see." Here I realize that birds have an advantage; they just preen themselves when they are ready to move on and say casually to one another, "All right, let's go."

March arrives to martial music; it's a warrior month; the winds are trumpets, the bright banners of the sky are unfurled, and the pennants of the clouds flutter. Now and again drums roll in an unseasonable thunderstorm, or the snow comes galloping in like white horses.

I listen for the song of the red-winged blackbird, wearing soldier's uniform, and watch for the first robin. Actually many robins winter on the New England coast, but none has stayed with me for some years, or if so, I haven't seen him.

My visiting robins send an advance scout, just one, a loner, as if on reconnaissance. He must go back and report that the food's plentiful and accommodations good, for shortly thereafter in will come a whole flock. When I see them, I think of the words of William Blake:

> A robin redbreast in a cage
> Puts all Heaven in a rage.

He was, of course, thinking of the English robin which differs somewhat from our own; but it was inevitable that homesick Britishers would name red-breasted birds—ours aren't as red as theirs—after their home variety.

When I reach the South, I will find familiar feathered creatures there—the robin, the mourning dove, the redwing, and of course some that do not come north to visit me, the mockingbird, for instance.

I spoke earlier of my Florida grandchildren's first flight. It was a turbulent one, but they were unconcerned. No one had told them there are good, bad, and indifferent flights, so they took the tossing in their stride and happily consumed breakfast. They thought that this was the way flying always is.

Innocence accepts and is not afraid. But people are always ready to prejudice the innocent. "Look," says a friend, "come to my house for tea next week. I have a classmate coming to visit me. You'll adore her." So you go convinced that you will, and it shocks you when you do not. Or someone else says, "Please go with me to this wretched party; you'll hate most of the people you'll meet, but I have to go and don't want to go alone." So you accept, certain that all will be quite dreadful unless you have sense enough to know that you are capable of forming your own opinions. Like as not, you have a wonderful time.

Emerson once said, "Though we travel the world over to find the beautiful we must carry it with us or we find it not." Perhaps the same is true of the ugly; not that we search for ugliness, but if it is within us, surely we will find it.

I believe that almost everything we discover in life is an extension of ourselves, often of the ego, but also of our spiritual awareness, which we may not even know we possess.

Look for tedium, and we'll find it; it's part of our equip-

99

ment; look for enthusiasm and we'll find that also; it, too, is in our personal luggage.

Speaking of luggage, I'll probably get mine down from the attic too far ahead. My folly is to pack in advance things I'll need before a trip and then have to unpack again. I always look forward to going south even if at the last minute something intervenes. I remember a time when I had planned a wonderful summer holiday, all beaches and dunes and bright blue water. And what happened? I went to the hospital instead. So a Cape Cod August was an unrealized dream, but October there has its own extraordinary beauty: warm days, as a rule, and red leaves lingering; frost-cool nights with stars as big as dinner plates; empty beaches with the summer residents gone, the children back at school, and the tourists from every state having for the most part headed home long since.

Plans alter in the tick of a clock and certainly at the onset of a fever. Maybe I'm growing superstitious or becoming cautious because nowadays I just say, "Perhaps," or "Maybe."

From one hour to the next a life may change. Several lives, often enough. But as I have thought and said for years, acceptance is a key to strength and practice makes it easier.

Just as compromise is necessary for much of living in amity with oneself, one's family, and friends, so is acceptance, and I don't mean only of the changes in one's personal climate, which is thermostatically controlled by the emotions, but the acceptance of the constantly altering world about us. Wherever I go people talk of change, and they are sometimes afraid and sometimes angry and always bewildered.

100

In my lifetime I have seen many changes, some of which appear to me to be good and some which do not. We can certainly accept the good and try to further it, each in his own way; and, with whatever weapons we possess, we can also fight the evils. It is not sufficient to deplore, fear, and rail against them.

Nostalgia is charming if it does not become a way of life. Too many of us, through memory and wishful thinking, try to escape into what we consider the good old days. It cannot be done, any more than we can return physically to houses in which we once lived happily, but which are now razed to the ground.

As a matter of sober fact, the past was never smooth sailing. We tend to remember the quiet waters and to forget the rough.

No era is without its inequities, its slow, or sudden changes, and every generation has known the fear, and anger, and bewilderment. It is a part of evolution. Nothing in nature stands still; though it seems to, as in winter, when we look at the bare trees, the going-forward is there, in secrecy and silence. Winter has work to do under and above ground, and this month we will perhaps see a little evidence of it, with more to come.

The world cannot stand still. It cannot sleep and dream old dreams. It must progress. Often the progression does not suit us, but we cannot halt it; we can only try, in our small way, to shape it closer to the ideal.

None of us can remain unaware of change, even if we cut ourselves off from all means of public communication, even if we shut ourselves indoors, draw the blinds, and refuse to answer the doorbell or telephone; we would be conscious of alteration, if only in the outward sounds and symbols, like the increased thunder of traffic, the

101

whine of power saws, the heavy advance of the bulldozer.

From time immemorial, people have complained that the seasons do not adhere to identical patterns, but indulge in variations. Last summer, for instance, in this locality, we experienced the driest August on record, during which the first of the hurricanes, petering out, dumped torrents of rain upon the not-too-distant South. I recall that my burning bush, some of the dogwoods, and other trees showed sudden crimson before September was a reality; the leaves of others, fatigued at the thought of making an effort, simply turned brown and drifted groundward. People, shocked by so early an autumn, began to dream of Indian summer, a short winter, and an early spring. For there is always hope.

March in northern New England, and other sections, is the month when the sap starts to run, though snow is still white in the woods; frost is an essential when the maples are tapped for their incomparable yield of sweetness.

Late or early, wet or dry, cold or warm, spring will come.

We must accept variation and, if we consider it objectively, mutation is welcome. If season after season exactly repeated last year's pattern, how monotonous it would be! And if our lives coasted along, without interruption or change, they might be secure but they, too, would be monotonous.

The Creator of all men and all things has provided the challenge of change, the necessity for acceptance, and variations in all patterns. We live by change, by struggle and the unexpected; for only in change, struggle, and the unexpected can we achieve growth.

Not long ago I asked a friend whose life had been abruptly altered what she was going to do. She answered after reflection, "God knows . . ." and both she and I believed He did.

Sudden changes in cherished plans are not the only factors that may prevent us from doing as we'd like. Few of us are free to come and go twelve months in the year. The vast majority have responsibilities and commitments, as well as necessary work. There are many reasons why we are kept on a short leash. Now and then we can slip it for a little while and lock the door behind us for a change of scene or tempo. I used to envy those who could afford the time and had the wherewithal to skip off at a moment's notice, go where they wished, and stay as long as they wanted, having made arrangements for the care of their houses and the discharge of their obligations. I don't think I do any more. The only time I ever did that, on my own—which is to say on a trip not mainly concerned with my profession—matters worked out very well. That time I went away not because I wanted a change, but in order to escape from myself, which, of course, I found I couldn't do; I had to travel with me!

Each of us manages some sort of escape I dare say. I find it, briefly, in books, old and new. I spoke a while back of the extension of the spirit; it can also be of the mind. This I am able to find in books that deal with subjects unknown to me and in the story of lives alien to my own. Yet no life, in whatever place or circumstances it is lived, is basically foreign, for all human beings have the same needs; all have aspirations, however one dream differs from another; and all know some measure of success and defeat.

The customs of which we read, the religions, the everyday conduct of someone else's household, the reactions of characters, real or fictional, reported by themselves or others, may seem as strange to us as if we were reading about people on another planet. Yet once we start sharing, the strangeness dims and the conviction of brotherhood emerges.

From childhood on, most of us desire to be different, to become individual. The pastor of my church once said that only successful people could afford not to conform to the usual pattern.

As a child, a girl, and even a young woman I always wanted to be other than I was . . . doctor, lawyer, explorer, reporter. I'd hear music and wish I were a musician, look at paintings and yearn to be an artist, watch a play and think I'd rather be an actress than anything else.

Now and then someone says to me wistfully, "It must be so exciting to be a writer!"

I don't think it's more exciting than any other profession. I do know some writers who appear to lead highly adventurous lives, but I'm not one of them.

Nowadays I never contemplate a visit to Tahiti in my daydreaming; but I still enjoy an unplanned picnic.

It occurs to me that I should keep a line-a-day diary. My mother did. When my sister and I closed her apartment, we found a small trunk filled with them. She didn't enter in her opinions, emotions, and such personal matters; she simply wrote down what sort of a day it was, and where she'd been and what she'd done. Actually one of these journals won a case for my lawyer father. I've forgotten the details, but the question centered around whether or not a certain man had called to see my father in his study at home, where he often talked with clients. My mother's diary was admitted as evidence and there it was, date and hour: At such and such a time Mr. So and So came to see Stephen at the house.

What I really should record is weather.

Remember I said that midway into January we still had had no snow? Maybe because I did say it, I remember that our first, if slight, snowstorm was the night of January nineteenth. We'd had a flurry or two during the day. Why do I remember? Because I was watching television and Gussie phoned me to announce it was "snowing like crazy" and I made a note of it. Before noon next day most of that "fallout" had vanished.

I cannot tell you what the weather will be like in Florida because I am writing this well before my departure. But it can be windy or calm, chilly or hot. One goes prepared; that is, I always think I'm prepared, but find, on arrival, that I'm not.

It will still be March when I return and I hope spring will have begun, even if reluctantly, even though Mr. Howells' lion-like month has tossed its snowy mane. In the South, spring comes earlier and more generously and as I expect to reach home at night I'll have to wait until morning to see if there are signs of life in the small bulb bed beneath the big south window. It's very warm there and sometimes there's a thrust of green even through snow. Later, growth appears in abundance, each flower, even of the same species, having its personal differences just as the birds do. They arrive, seemingly matched feather for feather, and singing the same song—yet, not quite. Surely each wild, winging bird has his own temperament. So each is, if almost imperceptibly, set apart from the rest of the flock.

It's the same with us. Let us say I have a friend whose ways are other than mine; we have our own likes, dislikes, prejudices, and enthusiasms. I like my steak rare, she prefers hers well done, so each considers the other in this unimportant respect a barbarian. I stay up late; she goes to bed early; I'm crazy about crossword puzzles; she

105

couldn't care less about them. We differ about some books, plays, television productions, colors, and fashions. Sometimes, of course, we agree. It's all trivial enough and we recognize our similarity, one to the other—and to other people. Differences make each of us himself, but likenesses make us part of a far larger world.

My friend and I have known anxieties, sorrows, and suffering; we are often insecure and troubled. We look upon the changing face of nature and may see different aspects of it, but we share, as we look. We can laugh or cry together and recognize the essential needs we also share.

So the difference makes us individuals, but the likeness makes us sisters.

When I come home, I'll have to start thinking about writing another book—a novel this time. I finished my last one a year ago this month. I haven't the glimmer of an idea, but I'm always hopeful that when I'm sitting in the sun, away from the typewriter and the big steel desk, and not thinking about work at all, an idea will come sailing into the unruly sea of my mind like a little cargo-laden ship.

Usually it does not.

Before I leave, as Honorary Chairman of our state Easter Seal drive, I'll be doing a little more than I have time to do. But it seems to me that when I'm pressured, when I haven't extra time, when I have what seem like impossible deadlines to meet, I manage. I regret to say that sometimes I have an entirely free day during which I could accomplish a great deal. On such days, feeling an absolute horror of going near the typewriter, I seem to accomplish nothing because I can say cheerfully to myself, "Oh, there's plenty of time," and so wind up after dinner with nothing done except perhaps the current mail.

Evidently I must have an invisible deadline breathing down my neck like a dragon.

I was interrupted a sentence or two ago by the unexpected appearance of my daughter and a friend. So, sandwich, cheese, fruit, and coffee for a scratch lunch and then the removal of a large heavy rug from the garage. I'd expected my daughter and her husband to come down for it tomorrow night.

Now I'm back at the desk again after about two and a half hours. Meantime the mail's in; I've washed up the lunch things, wandered out to the trash basket, and learned that a good friend is undergoing surgery.

Now, there are March birthdays to consider and I hope to be with the youngest Faith on hers.

Returning, it will be only a hop, skip and a jump to Easter, so I hope that March goes out appropriately like a lamb.

"I'll walk where my own nature would be leading . . ."

EMILY BRONTE

Mine at the moment leads me into April, but perhaps this is a good time to sit for a while on a bench outside some ancient English tavern, which I've never seen, or well protected against vagrant winds or snowflakes on the old lopsided seat by the almost waterless pond, a little way from the house, or even on a fallen tree in the damp, cold, and waiting woods where, despite any inclemency of weather, there is the smell of spring in earth still half-frozen, in boughs still bare, and the sound of spring emanating from a passing or pausing bird.

I listened not long ago to a wise and wonderful man say that when life became a little too much for us, we could find our retreat in an imaginary garden. He described one: flowers, fountains and quiet except for birds, and a reflecting pool, silvered with the last of a setting moon, then flushed with the rising sun, and in the pool flowers floating, opening to the dawn.

"Think of such a garden," he said, "and seek it in your imagination."

There are many gardens that I can visualize; one was in an oasis; one was once my mother's, crowded with old-fashioned bloom; another my sister's green garden as I saw it last summer.

Remember the garden Alice in Wonderland saw through the tiny keyhole and the difficulty she had in making herself the right size to enter it?

There are few people who cannot visualize gardens they have seen, others they have themselves planted and tended, or just the gardens they'd like to have. So, perhaps instead of woods and tavern or stone benches we'd better go into a garden.

It isn't easy, when we are pressured by a hundred things, to sit down quietly and dream ourselves among hedges and flowers and blossoming trees. Too much intrudes. Our scattered thoughts are like gnats, and we think of the eighty-six things we should be doing right that minute or of the hundred and two we've forgotten to do.

When I go upstairs this evening and attempt to compose myself after a busy working day interrupted by people and telephones, mail and obligations, I'll lie down for a few moments and try to think myself into the garden my friend described to several of us last week. An Oriental

108

garden, I believe; or into Esther's green garden; or into Gladys Taber's white garden with picket fence around it; long ago I had a tray luncheon there in spring, sitting in the sun. Or perhaps I'll think about a Virginia garden I once saw or a rose garden in Florida, or the moss garden, mainly moss and rocks, in Japan, of which I've only seen pictures. . . . Any garden.

I remember the one I had at the other house. We had a gardener then and a small green house. Before winter ended Henry used to bring me pages of requests for plants and seeds and such. And back in January my older daughter had written to innumerable places for catalogues and even seeds.

In the late winter and early spring everyone thinks of gardens if they have a little plot of land or a big one, a houseful of plants or just window boxes or geraniums in pots.

The geranium tree which Gussie grew for me—courtesy of a Florida friend of mine, a retired general, who grows hundreds of geraniums as a hobby and at my request sent me directions—is growing green and tall and will soon bloom again. One of the begonias she also gave me is flowerless, but has the loveliest leaves I ever saw. There is a special time in the morning when the sunlight slants in upon the table where it stands and polishes the leaves with gold.

Upstairs on the sun porch my African violets bloom, rest, and bloom again. I'm afraid I give them very little care. Agnes gave me a booklet on how to raise them, but when I read it, I despaired. So many instructions! It's like child-raising; if you followed all the instructions, you'd never have time to do anything else. So, as the African violets sit in the correct northeast light, all I do is give them a drink when they look thirsty, thank them for blooming, and when they don't, I inquire, "Are you just resting or have you given up?"

I admit that my thumb is usually stained with carbon or ink and isn't at all green, yet I am not quite happy unless I have some bloom, some bright leaves, some growth around me. I'd hardly say I live in a garden, but at least there are plants. I also admit that, except for the violets, I don't really take care of them. Gussie and Agnes do, and I enjoy them without responsibility.

Come April there should be more bloom, and I'll have seen my friend's rose garden in Florida and other lovely places, but always, in times of stress and disturbance, I'll try to think myself into a garden, a fictional one or real. For what is more restful and, in a way, out of this world?

Color and scent and silence; that is a garden, wherever it may be, remembered, seen, or imagined.

So between March and April we will rest for a moment in a garden, you in yours and I in mine, and while they may be very different one from the other, there will be no hedges or fences or stone walls between, so we can visit back and forth until it is time to continue our journey together into April.

110

April

"April's ivory moonlight . . ."

THOMAS BABINGTON, LORD MACAULEY

Ten to one you thought I'd use the well-known Sir William Watson quotation; I have, however, given you one from another of England's literary nobility. April is not all tears and laughter. She has her sober and thoughtful moments.

If June symbolizes the bride, May is a maid of honor, and April a shy, slightly nervous, quite unpredictable flower girl, who arrives with masses of forsythia.

There's a lot of forsythia on this property, over the stone wall above the road, by the kitchen door, and here and there in clumps, any old place. When we have had a prolonged warm spell in late winter, we can cut it and bring it into the house where it will bloom in a burst of sunlight in big floor vases on the hearth. One year I looked out of a window well past Thanksgiving and saw

111

it showing yellow. Now the blossoms scatter and blow across the steps and kitchen porch and lie on the ground like a yellow carpet.

Yellow is a delightful color if it hasn't that curious tinge of green which to my mind looks slightly bilious. I hasten to add that other people like it. I had a friend who loved both deep and pale clear yellows. They suited her nature, which was sunny. My mother loved it, too; her preference in bedroom decor was yellow and blue. My bedroom's blue and white, but the living room has the colors I feel so at home with: violets, mauves, pale and deeper pinks, aquamarine. One of my close friends not long ago surveyed my new pink curtains and thoughtfully remarked, "Why is it that I like green?"

This year Easter falls the day after my sister's birthday. She will feel cheated. She hasn't often had a birthday on Easter Sunday.

I always think of Williamsburg, Virginia, in April, for it was in that month I saw it for the first and last time. That April had decided to turn a cold shoulder, even in the South, but there was bloom and sunlight and, as I stepped from the car, a mockingbird was singing. I was enchanted by his song but somewhat less so when, for the duration of my stay, he—or perhaps it was a friend of his—sang outside my window practically all night.

That year Gladys Taber and Eleanor also came to Williamsburg and we made many little excursions together, looking at gardens open to the public, driving to the beautiful Jefferson mansion, and picnicking in the grounds of the house that had belonged to Pocahontas' husband. The grass was full of violets—the pale blue-gray and white variety—and we were permitted to dig up some plants to take home. They grew pretty well on my place but not nearly as well as at Gladys' where after all these years, they have spread and spread in the grass and on the terrace and by the well.

The custodian of the John Rolfe place sent me during subsequent years big boxes of cut jonquils from the grounds. I don't think Pocahontas ever lived in this house. She died, poor little princess, in Gravesend, England, a long way from home. Did you know that when she was christened, she was named Rebecca?

It was also the custodian of the Rolfe place, a charming woman, who told us how brick is laid. I remembered it for some time, and would astonish my friends by tossing my knowledge into the general conversation. I've forgotten it now, of course, though I dimly recall something about laid in bond (and I don't mean a secret agent). I just looked up bricks in the encyclopedia, but became confused, what with headers and stretchers and closers; however, I was happy to see my old friend bonding mentioned.

The first time I went to Mount Vernon was also in April. Later I was there when the roses bloomed and had luncheon under an ancient grape arbor with the delightful custodian of Mr. Washington's beautiful acres. I used to call him "the Colonel," and I wish I could find the book he signed for me. But hunting the needle in the haystack is child's play compared with tracking down a book in this house. I occasionally struggle to do something about this disorder; I endeavor to put the signed books on special shelves and alphabetically. I try to keep English unsigned books in one place and attempt to give nonfiction, travel, poetry their own lodgings. I don't succeed. The shelves are a perfect mishmash of books of different ages and sizes and I rarely find anything for which I look.

But I remember that the Colonel gave me a slip from a rose, purported to have been planted by George Washington himself. We brought it home and for a time it

113

grew, then disappeared. What happened to it I do not know; perhaps it was homesick for Virginia.

It grieved me to learn some time ago that Mount Vernon was in danger of losing its lovely view across the Potomac. So often nowadays, progress imperils beauty and history. Both should be preserved, for they are part of our heritage and should belong to our children and their children. It is true that all over this nation groups of dedicated people work to maintain scenic beauty and historical buildings. It was through the Mount Vernon Ladies' Association that I heard of the possible fate of Mount Vernon's view. And it's such a beautiful one. I saw it from the cupola, if that's the right term—I'd know if I could find that book—which had for some time been closed to visitors, but the Colonel displayed the view to me.

It seems to me that I remember a little swing door cut into the door of Mrs. Washington's bedroom so that her cat could come and go freely. But perhaps I dreamed it.

In any case, not enough people are interested in the preservation of beauty, despite the valiant efforts of so many groups. In recent years in New England I have witnessed history under the bulldozer and the destruction of so much of our past. Great century-old trees fall, and highways devour old houses. I suppose that it's more important that people have homes in which to live and roads upon which to drive than that birds have birds nests and that shade is shed on a blazing hot afternoon. Yet it seems to me that the planners for the present and future should somehow arrive at a compromise between the old and the new. For the past is an integral part of both present and future, and to erase it is to leave an incomplete pattern.

It's much the same with individuals. I've never ad-

114

vised living emotionally in one's personal past, with anger or resentment or nostalgia. Still, it colors all our today and influences tomorrow, but I believe that we can learn to look back with tranquility if lessons have been assimilated, the textbooks closed; and to remember the lessons with gratitude and serenity is an evidence of maturity.

We're shaped by inheritance and environment and by what we ourselves fashion from these. There was a period in my life when I spent a great deal of time indulging myself in futile regret. I thought (as many have thought before me and will think after me): If I hadn't done this or if I had done that . . . if I had spoken or if I'd kept silent . . . if only my decisions had been other than they were. I thought: If I'd just been patient and sufficiently wise and thus avoided mistakes which I recognized only after they'd been made, everything would have been different. Or so I thought then. But the hair shirt of guilt and regret serves no valid purpose. You have to discard it, and move on. As someone said to me recently in discussing her children's problems, "You can do only what at the time you think best."

Watching my grandchildren grow up—the oldest was married a year and a half ago—I pray that they will carry with them lifelong, the good, happy things, the knowledge of love and security, the joys of normal childhood and still recall with understanding the difficult times— for growing up is very difficult indeed—and so are the lessons learned while passing from one phase to another.

I have just made another attack upon the bookshelves; this was because a line of poetry came to me which appeared to fit in right here and in connection with my own remote youth—although it wasn't written about youth I am reasonably certain that I accurately recall the line, and almost sure that I know the writer's name. But I had to be absolutely certain and sure, as editors are very meticulous people, not to say fussy, and readers will pounce upon an error as a cat upon a mouse.

Speaking of mice, my groping through the shelves left me with the horrendous impression, brought about by an acute sense of smell, that somewhere in the walls a little creature has folded its paws and gone to sleep—not, thank heaven, near the desk this time. Twice before this has happened to us; once in the study in the other house and once right here in the walls by the fireplace, which is directly opposite me. Short of tearing down the house there is nothing one can do but suffer and wait.

So I'm back at the desk, none the wiser for my time out, and certainly a little apprehensive. Also my hands are far from spotless and if I don't wash them instantly, I'll leave the finger marks I hate all over the doors and woodwork. And I'm sneezing, for although the books in the study and living room as well as upstairs get a very good going over at stated intervals, it would be more than any of us could manage to dust them every day.

So back to my vanished youth without the quotation for which I have looked in innumerable reference books as well as anthologies.

I find that nowadays I rarely recall the past despairs and difficulties, the humiliations and disappointments, but that I do think often of the lovely moments when life seemed to surround me like a radiant light. I remember, too, the small, seemingly idle or unimportant moments—walking through an apple orchard or barefoot along a beach, standing beneath a palm tree in a picture-postcard sunset, or riding a little horse through early morning fog. I remember the wonders of small circuses under canvas, the excitement of the theater as the lights

116

go up, and many adventures lived in the pages of books, and always the companionship and generosity that have come my way. If at this moment I looked up to see a Time Machine standing here in the study, I would not enter it to press the button which would take me back. I am well aware that if I could thus live a large portion of life over, I'd make the same mistakes. No, I do not wish myself back in time; I recovered from that sickness of the soul years ago, but I'm glad that the good memories remain and have been sorted out so that I can see them in the proper light and perspective.

People often remind me, no doubt with the kindliest intentions, that I tend to forget names, numbers, grocery lists, and—if I don't write them down—even engagements. That's natural enough. You don't have to be my age to forget day-by-day things, the routine matters; sometimes you simply don't want to remember them. But lately, having grown weary of going upstairs at night and then coming down again, often even twice, for something I've forgotten to take up with me, I determined to save myself steps. So I've been putting things on the steps: a handbag, a box, a book. Trouble is I'm not likely to look down; my attention is fixed on the top of the stairs, so I'm apt to fall over anything in my path. Well, if this indicates a mental attitude, maybe it's worth a stumble or two.

When I think of the preservation of the good in the past, I think of this pleasing house. It's not in the least historical and it isn't old as compared to other houses I know, but it's been around, at least in part, since about 1800. I have tried to preserve it, but the mind and will falter and the budget screams when new cracks in the plaster appear in walls or ceilings, when window frames become increasingly stubborn and when I realize that I should bestir myself and have rooms repainted or repapered and

117

the outside done over again—white is a very vulnerable color. The indoor shutters, which close over the big living-room windows, are warping and tend to fly open when you least expect it and to bite the hand that closes them.

Old houses never let go of their past owners. I often think that while the many people who have lived here before me might not approve of, or agree with, my personal tastes or like the haphazard mingling of old and new I have round me, they'd tolerate my being here because of the affection I have for the house that once was theirs. In a sense, because I respect those who were born here, those who have died here, and those who have just moved away, it's still theirs, even now.

April is such a pretty name, I think. I know an April—and a great many Mays and Junes. Parents name their girl children for months, flowers, jewels, and there's a season which is popular in the record books. I know several women called spring. And there are Christmas babies called Noel and February children named Valentine.

However, I sometimes think that most children should be registered as Blank. (My sister was, our mother's doctor having thus entered the poor child in the records and when she went to get her first passport what a time she had. Blank Baldwin indeed!) I say this because so many children, and adults too, dislike their names; maybe they should be given a choice. And often the names turn out to be inappropriate or less attractive when the surnames alter. My father used to swear he knew people whose last name was Rose and who called their daughter Wild. That's very pretty of course, Wild Rose. "But," he'd go on, "she married a man named Bull!"

But April is charming and would probably suit any

woman who wears it. Aren't all women assumed to be unpredictable?

I don't know if I've ever reported how this place in which I live and the one before it got the name of Fable Farm. When I moved from New Canaan, I took the name along because it was a gift to me. I had for years known a man in California who, together with his staff, did the most magical things with letters and note paper. I remember ordering some as a present for Mignon Eberhart and he wrote to ask: What is her coloring? I told him and on the hand-painted sheets he turned out were pretty little girls in Sherlock Holmes deerstalker caps, examining things through magnifying glasses. Anyway, when I first moved to the country, he wrote me saying, "I hope you'll be happy at Fable Farm," and Fable Farm it still is.

Of course I started manufacturing fables long before I left the city and I've gone on doing so, year after year. It's been fun often and sometimes not, and it was pretty hard work, although no one ever thinks so—except myself.

I recently read a blasting review of my last novel. It ended by saying that I hadn't "the slightest idea of what made the masculine animal tick."

Maybe I haven't. And of many male novelists, far better writers than I, it's been said that they didn't know what makes women tick, either.

I grew up like most girls with men around me, a father, a grandfather, an uncle, cousins, and other relatives; later with a husband, sons, a brother-in-law and nephews, and now we've added some grandsons. I don't pretend to know what makes them tick. I get a clue now and then; we all get occasional clues. Few people see a man or woman whole, as it were. Everyone is something like a

119

diamond, all facets, and according to your relationship with him or her, you see one facet or several, but never all.

I dream up people for books and I try to place them in situations—growing out of the characters themselves—which would, according to my limited judgment, cause them to "tick" as I then report.

The writer obtains his material from life as he himself sees it. Most writers, like almost anyone else, have a rather limited view. Only the great talent and the rare genius can expand a viewpoint largely. Except in my youth I've not been guilty of trying to portray actual people I've known. But if I did, and you were that person, you wouldn't know it. For who can see himself through another person's eyes or imagination? Robert Burns said that a great deal better, long ago. Only if I set down specific events that have taken place in your life would you recognize yourself—and then only by these events. But I don't put friends or acquaintances before cameras . . . only a photographer can do that.

My older daughter and her family have for a little over a year lived in an upstate house once occupied by a writer of children's books. There are books written for children which I prefer to those written for adults. *Alice*, for instance; and the Mary Poppins stories; and of course *Wind in the Willows* and many others. When I was in my thirties, I collected children's books written by the English writer E. Nesbit. Many years later I found that Margaret Mitchell shared this passion with me. Most of the books weren't published here, but I found them, and was later able to share them with my children. But I read them first and perhaps enjoyed them more.

Anyway, my daughter's family now has access to about

ten acres and a sleepy little river; what nearby town there is you could put in a thimble, and the house must be permeated with the former owner's personality. Now that it's April I'll have to go up there again and see the changes that have been made. Gussie took me up last spring. It's so quiet there I think that at night you could hear a shooting star shoot!

Easter is early in the month this year and therefore it may be cold. But the storms should have passed. I can hear my Northern friends reminding me that one of their deepest snowstorms came on April eighteenth, but I'll ignore that. The sky should be blue except for those days when it decides to rain. And in this section how we wish it would!

I left the South blooming and it will go on doing so, but the North will just be thinking about and planning its early-spring decor.

Passover begins the night of April fifth; as usual, the Passover and Easter come close together. Each has its own solemnity, celebration, and beliefs, but each also stands for hope, trust in the Creator, and the promise of another spring.

It was Shakespeare who spoke of "the uncertain glory of an April day," but whether achieved by man or through Nature all glory is uncertain—except the eternal glory of God.

"Can two walk together, except they be agreed?"

AMOS: 3:3

Amos, who was among the herdsmen of Tekoa, was a minor prophet and, as I recall his short Old Testament

121

book, his predictions and revelations were usually gloomy, and his was a strong voice for social justice. I have, as usual, taken the quotation out of context and I've been sitting wondering how one could reply to that question, perhaps one might say, "Yes," and then qualify it by adding, "But not for long."

Such a question could be a postscript to a marriage ceremony or to the pledge of friends given one to the other.

However, there is solidarity; two can walk together and not always agree and even go for a time their separate ways, but return again to the common road.

It's not necessary always to agree with those you love; you can, like Voltaire, disagree but defend your companion's right to his opinion. I think the trouble with everyday disagreements with family and friends is that more often than not they become arguments rather than discussions.

My companion reader is in no way bound to agree with me as we wander through the years together. It would be difficult to agree with someone who, like myself, often contradicts herself. I thought just then of Walt Whitman's lines, "Do I contradict myself? Very well then I contradict myself," and feel somewhat cheered. But he went on to say, "I am large, I contain multitudes."

That takes thinking about, but I dare say we all contain multitudes . . . thoughts, opinions, emotions, ancestral heritages.

A friend stopped by a week or so ago and, looking at the papers scattered on the desk, asked idly, "Are you roaming through a year again?"

I suppose you could call it just that, and anyway no one, even while he is living it, goes right through a year on a ruler straight course, on a superhighway without a single turn, entrance or exit. We remove a sheet from a calendar every day or at a month's end, but we've not gone unswerving from one day to the next. The calendar reports one thing, but if we are honest, we must admit that we sometimes hurry and sometimes slacken, that we backtrack and that we try to cheat a little, going forward in our minds and mentally skipping a whole handful of days.

So on this little journey we wander, and I'll contradict myself, but there will probably be times when I can point out that occasionally October behaves like May or May indulges in a November mood.

Laurence Sterne spoke of himself as "The Sentimental Traveller," and this is a phrase I would like to pre-empt for myself. I don't know that I'd care to say I am traveling sentimentally through a baker's dozen of months, but rather that I am traveling with sentiment.

The path between April and May, the one not on a calendar, is brief. Which way shall we go? Shall we take a road through the woods that March has whipped through on gusty winds and April has prepared for her sister, the exterior decorator? Or shall we walk along a beach?

I like to walk where the tide has advanced and then withdrawn, where the sand is firm and wet and glistening, and to poke around in the cast-up seaweed for little shells and to search out those brought in on the high tide and stranded by the low. Shells are nautical miracles in their simple or intricate shapes, in their diverse coloring.

Much in little, and here we are back to Whitman: a thousand gardens in one garden, a million flowers in one flower, and the life, and sound, the scene, and color of the sea in one shell.

Just one of anything in Nature represents its species

and is wonderful: one garden, one flower, one shell; also one star, one snowflake, one drop of rain, one scoop of salt water from the ocean, or even one grain of sand.

Living in this beautiful complicated world, this restless and frightening and marvelous world, is to confront always the much in little.

It so happens that I like small things: miniature flower arrangements; little boxes, which I collected for many years; and I am perhaps fondest of the smaller mugs in the mug collection. I like (as a rule) small paintings and I enjoy small talk. This is not to say that I would want to live in a thimble; when it comes to rooms, I don't like mine small, though I don't want them so huge that I'm lost in them, and I like spaciousness outside the house as well as within. So there I go being contradictory again.

There's no reason why you shouldn't select your own road between the months; you can close the book and take off, and then later, I hope, rejoin me on this journey. Maybe you don't want to walk in the woods or on a beach. Perhaps between April and May you'd rather be sitting by a lake or a river or climbing a high hill or even a mountain with snow still on the peaks.

But whatever detour you may have made, come back with me when the path takes us into May.

May

"Therefore all ye that be lovers call unto your remembrance the month of May . . ."

SIR THOMAS MALORY

This is, of course, a reference to young lovers, also star-crossed lovers, but it holds for anyone who loves, for May is a month for young marrieds and old marrieds and for kith and kin and friends; it is also a month for people who are alone, for even lonely people must feel a lift of the heart if they are anywhere near a blossoming tree.

Now the apple blossoms on my ancient boughs blow rosy white in the May breeze. I've said it before and I'll state it again, May and October are my favorite months.

The poets, I find, are devoted to all the months, but April, May, and June seem to be their favorites. Shakespeare praised "the darling buds of May," but he also reminds us that they can be disturbed by "rough winds," and that "summer's lease" is short. But this is not yet summer.

125

More birthdays this month and my sister's anniversary. I'd like to hang a May basket on everyone's door.

Since I returned from the South I've hung over the half-moon flower bed, examined the trees, and held my breath, wondering how much has survived snow, ice, and drought. I'm astonished by the growth of some of the trees that need water and haven't had it. Dogwoods especially, but even if I could spare the well water, they are too far from the house (I cannot stagger distances with buckets) for the hose to reach. It won't be until later this month that I'll know how they came through. There were lots of the little gray buttons, which are the buds, last autumn. I'm hopeful, but not certain.

The will to survive in all nature is miraculous and a symbol of courage. Last autumn on Cape Cod I went outdoors to survey Gladys Taber's geraniums, for we'd been told there'd been a frost. They were bright, brave, and beautiful. And later in the Catskill Mountains, where I spent a day with my old friend Mary Margaret McBride I contemplated the small, creeping plants, outside the house which stands on a mountaintop and marveled that they were as green as if it were summer. Incidentally, I've no idea what they are called.

Man's instinct to survive is built in, but over the ages this has not been based solely upon primitive, self-centered instinct; as man evolved, progressed and developed, other factors entered in. And so he reached the stage where he wished to survive despite everything—pain, loss, and difficulties—because of much more than himself; he desired it for his family, who needed him, and for his friends, whose troubles and triumphs he shared, and for his work, which was of importance to him.

Then also, hand in hand with courage, he had hope and prayer.

Some time ago a young man whom I know and of whom I am very fond was stricken with an illness that for many years has been considered fatal. But medicine has crossed many frontiers and developed new techniques. Upon this hope he has built his life. Once released from the hospital, he took his wife on a wonderfully happy trip and then returned to work. He had complete trust in his doctors and faith in the future. This is not to say that he did not face reality, but to reality he added the magic qualities of determination and dreams. There were no traces of fear or self-pity, simply the will to fill every hour of his life with purpose, love, and with enjoyment of the world around him.

All those who know him owe him a great debt, myself included, for he has bestowed upon us a lift of the spirit.

Man always has struggled to overcome the obstacles, to escape the pitfalls and survive the dangers of living upon this earth; so do plants, trees, grass, and animals. All endeavor to adapt to environment and cirmumstances. I firmly believe that everything which has life and achieves growth possesses a philosophy.

Some time ago I met a houseborn quail. She was celebrated in her circle and far beyond it, and much has been written about her. But I was astonished to see her running freely around the house of her adopted parents —her "mother" was a lamp on the kitchen counter under which she was hatched—talking to them, and their guests, unafraid of a hearth fire, going for walks with her two human home-mates, greeting their friends and hers, and always showing very plainly her pleasure or displeasure. She was afraid of the birds that flew past her outdoors or swooped by the windows, for she hadn't the remotest idea that she was a bird. Only in one or two ways had

127

she retained the natural instinct of her species. It must have amazed her that the friends with whom she lived couldn't fly, for when they took her strolling, she'd fly up to a branch and then call when she was ready to come down and resume the little hike.

I used to send her postals, sometimes inquiring about her health, and it saddened me to learn a while back that she was no longer eating her little candies and scolding when the teakettle shrilled. But she had lived longer than quail born outdoors.

We have, of course, all known people who lived in dread, from moment to moment, but it has been my privilege to know those who at eighty or ninety or over, when they go to bed at night, are grateful for the day just passed and look ahead to tomorrow quite unafraid of it. Many of them had limitations, but they were solely of the body. Those of whom I now think—one was my grandaunt Charlotte, and another a marvelous New England surgeon—had no limitations of the mind or spirit; they retained a pure delight in living, humor, interest, appreciation of the world around them. I have often said that I do not wish to live to a great age, but the example of some of my friends has shaken the foundations of this statement. If the plan is for me to reach ninety and be unable to see, perhaps I can still hear; if I cannot hear, maybe I can see, however dimly. If I can't walk a mile or even a tenth of it, surely I can sit in a chair and remember, without resentment, the days when I could. Flowers afford fragrance which no one, however old or young, can see or hear; the sun brings silent invisible warmth, and the hand of a friend is something to which you can hold fast at any age.

"I'm deaf as a post," a friend wrote me a year or more ago, "and also otherwise handicapped, but I'm having a wonderful time. . . . I'm happy, taken care of, and interested in just about everything."

I'm twenty-odd years his junior and it's possible, as he's been very ill, that he is no longer living in the Mexican sun, but I know how ashamed that letter made me, ashamed of my frequent complaining, for he had learned the joy of living.

It is now time to walk in the fields and congratulate the wild flowers that have with mute determination lived through the winter, and to put my hand upon a blossoming bough, to look for a long time at the fruit trees, which are pink and white like the popcorn I used to string for Christmas decorations—and to be glad of life.

I'm not encouraged about my few roses. Two bushes were winter-killed the year before last, and I'm not sure I haven't lost another. I've no idea what June will bring me in the way of roses, but I always hope.

Now I can stop feeding the birds their especially mixed seed, for it's time for them to hunt their own banquets, although I do save bits of bread, cake, and cookies for those who like such treats because it attracts them to the feeders. They are, of course, busy seeking family houses or apartments. There are fewer birds than usual, I think. I haven't seen bluebirds or orioles on this place for far too many springs. Birds have always faced peril: animals that kill them or rob the nests of eggs; storms, car windshields, or bitter weather, but more menaces have been manufactured by man in addition to the natural ones. I am doubly grateful every time I hear a little song, see the shadow of wings, or catch a glimpse of bright color weaving through the greening trees.

Which reminds me, I must hunt up some yarn and hang it from a number of branches; some birds seem to

129

have a taste for color and so incorparte it into the nests they build.

We are born onto this earth to live for a short, average, or long time, and we have the ability to shape our lives for ourselves, despite the conditioning of heritage or environment and altering circumstances. As we mature, we come to the realization that certain events are as inevitable as dawn and nightfall; no one of us wholly escapes pain, none sorrow, and few fear. No life is exactly like another, any more than in a year's round each season duplicates last year's. This year's May will not be a carbon copy of another and even in the tropics, subtropics, and in the far north, seasons differ from those of other years, not in the main, but in detail.

A joy in living, a natural expression of the will to survive all personal disaster, can be constant despite whatever changes take place. Some fortunate people are born with it and others acquire it through learning and growth, achieving an intimate and individual philosophy. The happiest people I know enjoy intangibles as well as tangibles. They may look on the world through a window opening onto city streets, crowded and noisy—or upon a country road, the sea, the mountains, or meadows—but joy is within them, an integral part of their personal being. They delight in their families and their friends, they draw strength from a much-loved book or contemplation of a painting that has some personal meaning for them. I have a close friend who is moving presently from a big house to a smaller one which is being built; she is adamant about one thing—a painting which speaks to her in a quiet voice; whatever else the builder does, there must be in her new home a wall and proper lighting for this painting.

People who love intangibles can dream by a fire, they

130

can walk in the woods; tangibles are around them, the logs on the hearth, the living trees in the forest, but the voice which speaks to them from the heart of the fire or the trunk of a tree isn't tangible. They listen to music, which is a universal voice, and are comforted, uplifted, stimulated, or calmed. Each finds every day some delight which can sustain him through that day, and the night to follow.

May's sustaining gifts are blossom and birdsong.

Every now and then, quite by chance, I come on something which sustains me. Recently it was a little book called *The Fifteenth Pelican* by Tere Rios. This is a fantasy for adults. It is funny, touching, and enchanting. I have always loved fairy tales, best of all those which deal with magical matters involving not elves, gnomes, princes, and princesses but everyday people. The heroine of *The Fifteenth Pelican* is a very small, very real nun.

I suppose the reason I like books about ordinary people, involved in something which doesn't happen to many, is because I've always wished something other-worldly would happen to me. Now and then I believe it does.

That is my reason for rereading *Alice in Wonderland* and for reading books about animals that converse, not only *The Wind in the Willows* but many others; and for loving *Mary Poppins* and the books of E. Nesbit, whose fictional children are as real as the child next door, though the things that happen to them are utterly bewitching.

I managed to keep much of the big library I collected from an early age on. It has moved with me here and there and, as my children grew, I gave them many of the books; others they calmly appropriated—as for instance my E. Nesbits. I regret to admit that a number of my books were waterlogged, owing to my reprehensible

131

habit of reading in the bathtub. My mother wouldn't let me lock the door and she had an uncanny habit of popping in on me every now and then, so what could I do but hastily sit on the book and then busy myself with washcloth, soap, or back brush?

Eventually the books dried out, of course, but were never quite the same; the colors of the covers had run and there was a swollen aspect about them; but I could go on reading them, sometimes by flashlight under the bedclothes.

I am sorry for the child who does not grow into reading as he grows up; he has missed so much, and even learning to like to read in later life doesn't make up for it. I think my grandchildren like to read; I'm sure some of them do because I'm deluged with requests for Christmas or birthday books.

Last March I took to the Florida grandchildren two books written by a delightful couple, an artist and his poet and writer wife. I met them when I was part of a panel over in New Jersey last winter. I ordered the books when I came home and sent him bookplates to sign for the children. He not only did that but he drew, on narrow slips of paper, a pen and ink sketch of a small boy for the boy child, and a girl for the girl.

Several of the grandchildren now have autographed books. If I can manage it, I get such volumes for them—it's a wonderful thing to have a book you like signed by the writer. To start your own collection is pretty exciting. I was grown up before I had my first autographed book. I still have it.

Often I have lured a writer to my house, fixed him or her with a beseeching but determined eye, and put a pen in his or her hand. I remember the time, a great many years ago, when Naomi Mitchison came to New York from England. I practically dragged her to my house, and the poor woman probably had very little time for dinner because I had a great many of her books. The same was true of my dear friend Storm Jameson. I think the first time I met her was around 1948, although we'd written to each other for years. On the occasions when she's been in this country, I've kept her in a state of utter exhaustion, signing her name for me.

Writers have inscribed their books for me at autograph parties in bookshops and department stores, at authors' luncheons and dinners. They've also answered my letters and their replies are pasted or taped in their books—if they did reply; they don't always.

I had one friend who autographed his first book for me, with an inscription in Persian. He then wrote a translation of it. The translation was flattering in the extreme and for days I went about swollen with vanity until it occurred me to ask myself: How do I know what he wrote in Persian? I had nothing but his word for it that the translation was correct (incidentally, he wasn't Persian).

He's gone now, as are many of the writers whose inscriptions are in books on my shelves. But they live in their books; in the words they wrote down just for me, some as long as fifty or more years ago; and in my memory of them personally.

I seem to have wandered away from May, but if ever a month was meant to set you wandering, it's this one.

Now and then in the spring a friend sends me a carefully packed little tin of arbutus, and I put the flowers in a small mug and rejoice. It is scarce nowadays and is protected in most states. The blossoms look like dawn-flushed, very tiny stars, and each star holds heaven's own unique faint fragrance. I've never seen arbutus grow in my section of this state. It must have been plentiful on Long Island in my youth. When I was a girl and happily played a terrible game of golf there, I had a girl caddy. I think her name was Henrietta, and she was a native of Shelter Island. Long after I was married, when my summers and springs were lived in a busy city, my friend used to send me arbutus.

Trailing arbutus, the May flower, does not stun you with a spectacular show of blossom. It creeps quietly along the ground and does not advertise itself; you have to search for it, as you do for many rewarding things.

In Australia there's a flower called boronia, I think. The blossoms, as I recall them, are insignificant, but the scent is marvelous. They used to make a perfume from them, which I've had, but to my mind it never quite captured the real fragrance.

Now it's May in Australia but not spring, just as it isn't spring in South America. But our own South is teeming with it.

In Hawaii they will have celebrated Lei Day, and the scent of gardenia, tuberose, ginger, and dozens of other blooms will be on the bright-blue air; the shower trees and the jacaranda will have blossomed. I remember standing in a certain spot in Hawaii and looking at the sea and at snow-capped mountains through rows of jacaranda trees, the blossoms of which are not quite blue and not quite lilac.

Also in Hawaii there is a little green leaf with a marvelous scent. I have forgotten the name and my friends who were born there or who have lived there are not within reach of my telephone at the moment. I know that the little leaf is woven into leis, that it supposedly has magical properties, and that the odor is wonderful.

The nearest I've come to May in England was the first

week of June. I'd like to be there when spring comes early and the hedgerows blossom and as Tennyson wrote, "The world is white with May." Hawthorn is called "May" and I love it. The pink and white and the dark red. I had a hawthorn tree on the other place, the blossoms like miniature roses; and one stands at the entrance to my church. Until a hurricane struck and the sea came in, my sister had a good many.

I don't like to leave May, or to have May leave me. . . .

There is a quotation from Swinburne's "An Interlude," which says:

> And a bird overhead sang *Follow*,
> And a bird to the right sang *Here*;
> And the arch of the leaves was hollow,
> And the meaning of May was clear.

I haven't looked up the whole poem so what Mr. Swinburne meant, I don't know. I just hope that to you, and to me, the meaning of May is clear.

"Time travels in divers paces with divers persons."

SHAKESPEARE

In the scented moment between May and June I would halt time while I myself travel, and one path I would like to take is to my sister's. The place she calls Homeport is on a big, fresh-water pond made beautiful by

135

many swans; not far from the pond is the beach and beyond the beach is the sea. Spring comes earlier in southern Connecticut than it does to the eastern end of Long Island, and when I go to Homeport the laurel will have been in full bloom here, but just coming into blossom there.

In the morning or late afternoon I like to walk to the beach through the woods, which in June will be full of wild rocket, or through the green garden, and then take a short cut through bushes or take the meadow way. Wild roses and lilies of the field and all manner of flowers are in the meadow and the pond banks are thick with *Rosa Rugosa* and honeysuckle.

By whatever path you select, eventually you reach the small beach and the boathouse, and look back across the pond to watch the swans rise in sudden flight, the wind in their wings creating a special song.

I sometimes think that wherever we are, physically, we are often too busy fully to enjoy it, whether we are visiting or touring, whether we are at home or abroad. But if, during a cluttered day or crowded evening, we have five or ten minutes to spare and can stand by a window or sit in a big chair and with the broom of the individual will sweep the cobwebs and concerns from our minds, we can go somewhere in memory and for a little while experience a delight which, were we transported there in the flesh, we might not wholly realize.

It's a good thing to know that places we've been remain with us life-long, if we so desire; even if we don't, they are there in the subconscious. This is not to say that there aren't for all of us places, times, and events to which we'd rather never return. But we need not deliberately take ourselves on the journeys which end, not in lovers meeting, as Shakespeare said (he said practically everything, didn't he?), but in disappointment or disaster. Given the will power, we can cull over memories as one sorts out fruit, discarding some, tossing away others, keeping only those which reward us.

I'll make you a wager; if in June I walk to the beach or stand on the bank above the pond, or pause at the trellises to see which roses are in bud, I shall not have greater pleasure than at this minute, miles away from Homeport in my house. For I'll be thinking of other things then, even while admiring flowers and trees and water. Perhaps my sister will have sent me to cut some mint or parsley or remove the covering from her beautiful tiled table on the little brick—what is it, a miniature patio?—in the green garden.

We are always so concerned and involved with the things we are doing, or with the things we are going to do, that it is difficult fully to savor each moment, as bright, as fleeting, as fragile as the soap bubbles we blew when we were children.

If I look at my calendar, I see there the accurate undeviating dates: Tuesday, May thirty-first, says one page, and the next, Wednesday, June first. There's no time between pages; one follows the other inexorably. There isn't a blank page between which says, "Wait a little; pause here."

But the human mind is not an assembly of three hundred and sixty-five or -six pages. It makes its own chronicle. There are dates that are never torn out and thrown away, and dates the mind deliberately omits; the almanac of the mind is a collection of days and weeks, months and years, which go backward or forward as the mind determines; a record that is sometimes crowded and that sometimes exhibits gaps.

So, despite what my desk calendar says, or the dish-

137

cloth one that hangs on a wall of the tiny pantry, I am making my own pause between May and June and I hope that you will, too.

I used to think, as a child, that if you crossed from one state to another they'd be immediately and noticeably different, for in my geography books each had its own color. I was quite astonished when, at a very early age, I was taken from New York State into New Jersey. I don't suppose I expected borders and customs for I knew nothing about those, but I did anticipate a sharp alteration in the landscape and even the color of the earth. But, of course, it's only as you travel farther into another state that you begin to see such differences.

It's the same with the seasons and months. You might think that, going to bed on the last night of May, you'd awaken on the first day of June to an altered world. But you don't. The weather may be almost the same, and you may have to travel deeper into June to discover the changes.

My daughters had a strange little custom of pronouncing a small spell when awaking on the first of any month and then, if my memory serves me, of going downstairs backward. I assume that this was intended to bring good luck, but it could very easily have brought bad—a broken leg, for instance—although it never did.

Now that we have paused for a brief moment of our own making, we can draw a deep breath, leave May behind us, and go forward into June.

June

"In the leafy month of June . . ."

COLERIDGE

This is the month of brides, roses, graduations, and anniversaries. In my circle of friends and relatives—that always seems a silly way to phrase it. Can't relatives be friends, too? Of course they can—there are also birthdays.

In this hemisphere May and June are favored months. Most of us harbor slight—or profound—reservations about the other ten—too hot, too cold, too stormy, too dry, too chancy. But even June has her uncertain moments.

I can recall one June so cold that we lighted hearth fires in the country and kept stoking the furnace, though the May which had preceded it had been so hot that everyone panted, melted, and complained. The tenth of that month was my sister's wedding day, so I well remember.

I sometimes think of March as a blustering, lively un-

139

predictable little boy; of midsummer as a sleepy housewife; of the autumn months as gypsies, but the spring season is composed of young girl months!

Last year I went to my sister's on the eighth of June; this year I'm not sure on what date I'll go. This annual visit stimulates my mind and greatly refreshes my heart and spirit. I can't say that I'll relax much physically, for Esther is a very active person, and she usually plans a daily project or two not only for herself but for me. We race around much of the time and keep extraordinary hours, and we don't always agree, which is as it should be. Look at the birds in their nests assumed always to agree. Ha! Have you ever watched them pushing one another out of their little shelters and quarreling over food before they learn to fly?

My sister and I do not push each other out, nor do we squabble over bread crumbs and bird seed—she is, incidentally, a fabulous if sometimes slightly demented cook—but occasionally we differ and this is fine; a healthy discussion every so often is essential to any relationship.

I look forward to seeing my brother-in-law on weekends. I don't see him as a rule during the rest of the year, so this is a delightful fringe benefit.

Last year one of my nephews and his wife were at Homeport for two weekends. They left baby Susy with us during the week and my sister had an enchanting college student baby sitter.

In June the roses on the wall of the brick terrace start to bloom. I think they're Doctor Van Fleets, but I'm not sure; I'll never reach my sister by telephone today to have her confirm this, and the name doesn't much matter; there are masses of them along the top of the wall and cascading over the side, and the color is heavenly.

Sometimes when I reach Homeport early, they are just

140

in bud and I inspect them every day, as if I were paid time and overtime to announce the first sign of color and the first grand opening.

No matter what happens in the slow-swinging circle of a year, we seem always to have something to which we can look forward—a visit, a holiday, a tree coming into leaf, a flower giving its heart to the sun, someone's birthday, or graduation, or just June itself.

This is the burgeoning month, bridal white, blush pink, deep pink, apple-jade green; and the month when roses kindle along bough and bush or over wall or trellis in little flames of pink, flushed white, deep red, crimson, and scarlet. It is also the month of going ahead and stepping into the future. It always makes me think of young people who leave school for college or college for the plunge into the working world and of brides who float down aisles. It's a new year, in a sense, young June.

June is like a girl on the brink of new adventure with her short past behind her and her future ahead. June is youth. It often saddens me that the young must grow older, but there is so very much to learn in the process. It's not such a long step really from the diploma to the office, from the wedding cake to the responsibility of running a home and raising a family. June opens many doors to those who walk through her dazzling days, hoping so much, fearing a little, and with their hearts on tiptoe.

I've seen my own children graduate, the girls from school or hospital training, while the boys have gone to war and returned to seek further education or to work. Always we pray that all will be well with them—not only at graduations, and homecomings or weddings.

From the finite viewpoint things never seem to even

141

up. We appear to have too little of this or too much of that. Whether it's the outdoor temperature or the climates of our personal lives.

I try—not always succeeding—to think, to wait and see. Storms subside, and there are periods of calm, and if we look only for evil, we forget the balancing good.

No one, not even the June young-married or the graduate, was intended to live a life of quiet ease, coasting along in complacent untroubled monotony, one day slipping into the next. That's not only monotony; it's worse; it's strangulation. Sometimes we say, "Oh, she has everything!" It's never wholly true; no one has, really. Also we say, "Well, there's a completely happy family," and that's not quite true either!

We learn from joy but also from grief; we learn from achievement, but just as much from failure; and what we learn from grief and failure is, after a while, to be grateful. To the young person this may not seem a verity. But it is. I believe that all of us, young and old, learn more from obstacles than from the smooth path and from bracing ourselves against sudden harsh winds than from the undisturbed weather.

So the graduate and the bride, walking her rose-petaled way, learn more from change and challenge than from dreaming; not that dreams aren't important. But rewarding dreams must challenge and be fluid enough to shape, as nearly as possible, into reality.

We have waited through the long winter and the uncertain spring for June to come and bring us the splendor she has hoarded for us; now she spends it and, if she's true to her usual pattern, lavishly. Even when she's moody, June keeps most of her promises.

For those who look upon this month as a gateway to a new life and to opportunity, we all wish good and happy

142

things: new roads to explore, higher hills to climb, and strength to meet whatever is to come; and for those to whom June is an old story, we wish that they may experience every now and again a flash of that young wonder which once was theirs.

Not all June winds will be gentle and not all June days fair, but there's bound to be sunshine and there are always stars.

Last winter when June was several months away, whether you looked ahead or back, I heard from one of my readers. She was eighty at the end of last October, and she wrote me that she had driven to Florida alone from Michigan and was happily settled in a trailer; her new neighbors were kind, and their interests were much like her own. I nearly collapsed when she told me of the long drive, but there was "more to come." She'd been dancing once or twice a week, learning new steps, and she said that she "did as well as anyone else" and people seemed to like to dance with her!

I wondered how she'd happened to think of sending her letter to me in care of the Library of Congress (it reached here very quickly) and decided I'd better stop talking about growing old.

Before I go away the half-moon garden will have bloomed; it does so very early. There won't be daffodils and tulips, but the japonica and my one laurel bush will have blossomed, and I never know how long the lilacs will linger. Funny, from one year to the next I can't remember normal blooming dates, and I've given my gardening books away. Agnes usually gives me pansy plants on Mother's Day. The sweet-scented viburnum may come earlier than June, I can't remember. Perhaps it's good to forget; then you don't brood over your bushes, trees, and flowers and scold them for being too early or

143

too late. When they do come into flower, you are delightfully surprised.

I never tire of seeing, if I rise early, the sparkling dew upon the grass. Even when, as in recent years, our grass has mostly been missing, there's dew on boughs and weeds and flowers. I think dewy is a charming word; just as misty is. I often run across the word roric as a definition for dewy in crossword puzzles. I don't like it as well. I am very fond of words in general; in particular, there are some I love and some I heartily dislike, and some, with similar meanings, about which I'm selective. I like lonely, for instance, better than lonesome.

Perhaps my sister will let me do a puzzle with her; she's generous about puzzles. Gladys Taber and I do them, too, but Gladys guards hers jealously. Once in a while, if she is in the study wing, working and I'm alone in the living room I sneak over to her special place on the couch and steal the clip board to which a puzzle is always fixed. Then I put in a word or two, hoping I can solve something she hasn't. When she returns, she regards the clip board with a lifted eyebrow and is quite happy, I think, when she determines that my word is incorrect and then, gleefully, erases it.

I know one man who, his wife says, attacks her current puzzle with a pen; I heard of another just the other day. This is really the height of self-assurance. I don't know what I should do without an eraser, and this applies not only to puzzles, but to practically everything from my work to my memories.

I put out the yarn for the birds as I said I would, and some of it has been picked up. Now and then I see one flying past with a thread of blue or yellow, pink or red streaming from his beak like a little banner. I never see the nests into which this gaiety is woven. I

144

wonder if orioles would use yarn? I had many orioles on the other place, and we had some which returned every year to my parents' house on Shelter Island. One pair built near the house in an old pear tree, and my father used to sit on the porch and watch them through binoculars. You could see any bright strange pattern in such a nest, one of the most intricate of all built by birds.

I can just hear the female of the species saying to her mate, "I'm awfully tired of just twigs and grasses and the general uninteresting color. I'd like to change our decor; it's so boring to fly back to a nest that is like almost everyone else's. Let's try a bit of whatever that is on the bough over there; at least it would brighten things up."

Now is the time when if I walk by the dunes and along the beach, the sea is often troubled and restless—and very cold—but there are days when it's almost as undisturbed as Georgica Pond and lies almost as quietly, milky blue and opal, under the sun.

I must admit that I do not now go swimming in the Atlantic, and it's been a number of years since I braved even the warm Pacific in Hawaii. I don't like cold water; I don't like rough water or big waves; and I don't like undertow.

Last summer I merely watched when, early in June, youngsters romped in and out of the icy water, as did their elders. As a girl and young woman, if I were near a body of water—lake, river, pond or sea—I felt obliged to enter it, no matter how cold it was. Not now. I decided a number of summers ago that I had reached the time of life when I could stay out of blood-curdling water no matter how my friends pled with me. After living for a considerable time in this world I believe one is entitled to reject a few things. . . . I no longer climb windmills or ladders, trees or mountains; nor do I endeavor to skate

145

on glassy ice. I no longer am compelled to dance all night or hike all day or camp out or brave a snow or sleet storm. I don't have to any more. That's one of the compensations of growing older. There are deeds you need not perform, merely to prove you did once upon a time. I have totally erased such antics from my schedule.

Now we go toward the longest day; maybe I'll be home then, maybe not, generally we don't think much about the day which leads us into summer, as most of June is still spring. Nor do we stop to consider that immediately after the longest day, the days begin to shorten.

The full moon comes early in this month, but should I be on Long Island after it's waned, there are still the rather eerie but enchanting floodlights which irradiate my sister's bushes and lawn, meadow and trees.

I've looked in the almanac to learn something about June's evening and morning stars, but I always become hopelessly enmeshed in astronomical terms. Still I believe that in June I'll be seeing Jupiter above the horizon at sunset. I'm not as apt to be up at sunrise to greet the morning star. I suppose on those far-away occasions when I did dance all night I have seen it a time or two.

Last winter when we had storms, or the clouds which presaged them, I used to go upstairs to the sun porch and look in vain for the evening star. In clear weather it would remain for a while, after coming up out of the sunset and rising, increasingly brilliant, in the darkening sky. I missed it when I couldn't see it or when I came upstairs from work and it had already set. It always gives me a sense of companionship almost as if I owned a twinkle of it. I look up from a book or away from the television set and there it is beyond the window following its own course and pattern, moving toward its setting.

The day during which I've been writing this has been a particularly difficult one. This morning there occurred one of those complete—maybe nervous—breakdowns in the household machinery and men have been swarming busily about since before noon, outdoors and in. It's now four in the afternoon and they have just departed. Also I found myself the victim of what may have been a very unpleasant practical joke; if it were intended as such, whoever perpetrated it has a perverted sense of humor; but I believe it was done out of malice, something I've rarely encountered, and it frightens me.

Still the day is close to being over, and I can compose myself this evening and look for my steady shining star.

Recently while hunting up something in an anthology I came upon a few lines I'd not read before; I like them and hope you will.

They were written by Richard Trench, Archbishop of Dublin, who was born in the year 1807 and died in 1886. and are from a poem called "The Kingdom of God":

> I say to thee, do thou repeat
> To the first man thou mayest meet
> In lane, highway, or open street
>
> That he and we and all men move
> Under a canopy of love
> As broad as the blue sky above.

I'll try to remember that whenever I've been inconvenienced or there have been delays and annoyances, and even if I should once again be distressed by the mischief, or malice, of an unknown stranger.

Gladys Taber often uses a phrase that remains with me. Before we went out she'd carefully list the errands we had to do and the friends we were to see, and as we got into the car she'd say something like, "Then when we come back, and before we go to Millie's, we can take Holly for a run on the beach; and there might be time to stop by and see Helen, and still come out even." And when we finally returned home, if we'd succeeded in our endeavors, she'd say triumphantly, "See? We did come out even!"

Yet she'd left it flexible. Sometimes we didn't quite make it, but she knew that on the list there'd be something we could catch up with the next day.

I've been saying for a long time that in the celestial plan things adjust so that the books balance. I know it doesn't seem to work that way in our personal accounting, but when I begin to fret over my own shortages and debits I'll remember the Bishop of Dublin's "canopy of love" and stop complaining.

I am as my friends know, a talented complainer, and one of them said to me not long ago, "Well, at least you never have a dull moment"; and I answered passionately, "But, how I wish I did."

Actually I don't think I'd care for dull moments, just for quiet ones, and there are always a few of these in a week's time or a month's passing. The trick is to appreciate them and not to take them for granted.

We take too much for granted; the air we breathe, for instance, or the flowing of water through a faucet. It is only when we lack these that we recognize their value. All of us have experienced coming into some small, almost airless room, or being knocked over by a wave in the ocean, or falling into a body of water when we are unable to swim; the first breath we can take thereafter is pure wonder. All of us have had the very ordinary experience of having household water cut off by a power failure, or a difficulty with a pump or a well, or just a

148

time when, because of repairs, the water must be cut off for an hour or more.

We also take friendship for granted; and love, itself. The love of those close to us; the love of God, the canopy.

The quiet moments pass quickly and we go about our daily routines, forgetting to be grateful for the few small but important moments when as Whitman said we can "loafe and invite" our soul.

Every year we encounter difficulties; we come face to face with illnesses, financial trouble, or grief and in a year's time there are many crises. But I doubt if God's plan and Nature's is measured into days, weeks, and months. It's the long range, the over-all schedule. Therefore if you look back, not over the weeks but years, I think you'll find that, after all, things did come out even.

For every friend who has failed us there is one at least who stood by; for every sorrow there is a time of happiness, and for every disappointment, a new opportunity.

All this month June will go her careless yet ordained way, with July treading on her rosy heels. So between now and tomorrow, before we cross the imaginary line between one month and the next we can linger for a moment and realize that June came out even, and so I hope, did we.

"Time has fallen asleep in the afternoon sunshine."

ALEXANDER SMITH

Last night I was watching television, without a star to guide me, and a friend who telephoned asked what I was

149

looking at. I told her and she said, "I thought you more sophisticated than that."

Oh, well, many of my friends deplore my sometimes light-minded choice in viewing. But the term sophisticated amuses me. I became tired of it long ago because people employed it to describe everything from other people, to prize-winning poodles, clothes, attitudes and tastes, interior decoration, bath towels, or food.

So I looked it up in my Oxford Abridged.

Actually it derived from sophism, "a clever trick or device, specious but fallacious argument used deliberately to deceive or mislead." Among other things, sophisticated means "adulterated" and not genuine. My Oxford does not sanction the way we employ the term, but other dictionaries must because it's come by usage into the language; anyway, considering the original meaning, I'm quite pleased when I am accused of a lack of sophistication. My friends, of course, ponder what must be my low IQ. I wouldn't know.

I've lived through a lot of catch phrases. I remember how, some years ago—when lay people became exposed to psychological and psychiatric terms and began using them in everyday speech not really knowing what they were about—everyone thought himself "sophisticated" when he could fling around terms like "complexes."

More recently we have all become status conscious, although "status," medically, refers to an abnormal state. It also has legal and financial meanings as well as indicating merely position or standing in society or a profession.

Now everyone talks about images, which once meant simply "an artificial representation of the external form of any object especially a person." So that too has gone through a lot of definitions.

Me, I like coined words that don't alter or end up very far from the original meaning. Take serendipity.

Horace Walpole coined that back in 1754 when he wrote the fairy tale, "The Three Princes of Serendip," which was the old name for Ceylon. The princes during their adventures kept making "discoveries by accident and sagacity of things they were not in quest of" so serendipity means "the faculty of making happy and unexpected discoveries by chance."

We all do that, and serendipity is a delightful name for it. So during this little pause between months we might consider our chance discoveries, material or otherwise, while we sit for a moment and look at the foliage which is beginning to thicken on the trees and to lose that very youthful June green.

Finding material things is a sort of serendipity. Once with a friend I was at a shrine situated in the midst of many acres. We'd been walking and sat down to rest on a stone parapet. I was looking idly about and listening to a bird sing, when I saw something shining in the sun. After a while I got up to inspect it—a piece of mica, I thought, or a bit of tin foil. But no, it was a little deep pink heart, it could have been lost from a bracelet or child's necklace. It was without value and very pretty. There was no way to trace the owner. Hundreds of people came to this place every week; no one that I knew of ever advertised for it; a little heart-shaped piece of glass. But I was enchanted by it, shining there almost at my feet upon the well-worn path.

Often driving somewhere with friends I see something I don't expect to see, and so haven't looked for—like the kangaroos I saw in the glare of headlights one dark night in the Australian bush, or the doe and fawn I saw come down to the water on the beach at the Cape.

A while ago I went to the city—I rarely do any more, having grown to dislike it—to spend an evening and a night with my friend and agent, Dorothy. I hadn't seen her for a long time before that; mostly we talk by telephone. I came into town around five and went to her apartment; and after a while we went out to dinner. It was a wonderful occasion for we had perhaps two years' catching up to do; not talking business, not in an office, not conscious of a limited luncheon hour. No one was with us. The only people we saw were just strangers in a public dining room.

The next day was Armistice Day and the city was quieter than usual; we rose late, went to lunch, and I took a train home. It was pure serendipity. I'd expected pleasure in our meeting but not the relaxed time of laughter, discussion, and remembering.

I often think of that and of that other serendipital occasion when, almost upon the spur of the moment, we took off for the Berkshires together, a little trip that hadn't demanded a great deal of planning. As a rule I plan far ahead. One of my closest friends often tells me I am too organized (she's pretty well organized herself, being a perfectionist, which I'm not), so I suppose that any occasion when I don't plan ahead but go somewhere or do something unexpected, is a sort of serendipity.

Gifts you don't expect can be serendipity. You're certainly not looking for them. For instance, last winter someone sent me masses of shelled pecans from her daughter's grove; and she'd managed to do this almost on her way to the hospital for surgery. I wasn't expecting a present on that particular day. I was looking only for the morning mail, routine letters and even more routine bills, but I found the unexpected.

152

All of us possess the faculty of the three princes for finding along the way pleasant things for which we are not looking. Perhaps in July in addition to those things we expect we will find serendipity on our paths.

July

"All the live murmur of a summer's day."

MATTHEW ARNOLD

Last January I made a little vow. I told myself: No matter how hot it becomes next summer, I will not complain but remember the bitter cold last winter, particularly that end-of-January storm and the night the furnace blew up!

But, I'll probably forget . . . anyway I wonder why many household mechanisms, such as furnaces, go wrong when it's zero weather, and also usually on a Sunday?

Now we have the evenings, long and lingering, when, after the sky darkens and the lamps are turned on, the fragile moths shatter themselves against the big windows and screen doors, trying to beat their way to the light. So I close the inside shutters in the living room and the wooden doors.

I am aware of nocturnal creatures—koalas in Australia, the moles which hump up what's left of lawns, and of whippoorwills, owls, and little furry hunters. There was one night bird that used to cry out for hours in the trees on the Cape. I never knew what it was.

Most of us, however, need light. Many things, especially the moths and flowers, often the birds, and always human beings, seem to seek light. It was the dying Goethe who said, as his mortal sight dimmed, "More light!"

The July light here is heavy and golden; the month is often relentlessly hot and we do have humidity. I don't know what will happen this month, but I'll try to remember January, and to accommodate myself to blazing noons, breathless afternoons and nights. Now the leaves droop and scarcely stir, and dust settles on them and birds hide in the deeper, cooler woods, coming out only as the sun lowers, and then singing their hearts out until bedtime. Often something wakes them during the night and they chirp sleepily and briefly, enchanting me with a liquid phrase or two, if I am also wakeful. Sometimes also during the night I hear an owl, and for owls I have a real passion.

July is a radiant month; the stars blaze, and on the Fourth rockets will soar and shatter into little stars, falling earthward. The full moon is on the second this year, so fireworks will have to compete with her. Even as a girl, moonlight turned me melancholy rather than romantic, but it's a pleasant melancholy. I sit on the sun porch, if I'm at home, and look out, when the time is right, to see the moon soar slowly through the branches of the huge old mulberry tree and then sail unencumbered, into the dark blue heavens attended by the stars.

I don't know where I'm going this month. I have to work, of course, but I'd like to steal a little time and fly to Colorado to see my younger daughter. I was once with her in Denver when they had what was for that section unusual weather; it was as hot as it has ever been here.

I remember because I was briefly ill and imprisoned in a hotel room and Ann would come panting in to inform me that even a mile-high city could swelter.

This is a favorite vacation month; people will be going to various places, full of plans and anticipation, and still others will be returning home sun- and wind-burned, remembering all they've seen and done.

Most vacationers will also remember the things they forgot to pack for the lake or mountain, river or seashore; the clothes they should have brought for cruise or plane or train; and after they return will also recall things left behind in rented cottages or hotel rooms.

I'm stubborn. I don't have to go anyplace to leave things. As the years go on, my inborn talent for mislaying objects becomes more marked. I strew handkerchiefs as the wind strews leaves and I think my glasses, regulars as well as spares, sometimes develop feet and just stroll away from desk or bedside table. Of course, I have a horrid habit of casting them down, on couch, or bed, or bookcase. I remember that once, after the house had been hunted over, I actually opened the door of the refrigerator, and peered into it. I wish I could report that I found them sitting on the shelf next to the milk, but I didn't.

Perhaps I am a reincarnation of *Alice in Wonderland's* White Rabbit. I drop gloves as he did and hurry about, muttering to myself, "Oh, dear; oh, dear." I still ascend the stairs in the evening complacent and tired, certain all's been done that should have been, and then toil down again looking for something I absolutely must have. It's on such occasions that I remember two things I have neglected during the day. I don't know why it's always two. I just went upstairs and fetched a copy of *Alice* and checked. The Rabbit also said, "The Duchess, the Duchess! Oh, *won't* she be savage if I've kept her waiting." A little later, still keening about the Duchess, he added, "Oh my dear paws! Oh my fur and whiskers!" For he'd lost his gloves.

I don't see why the Great Intellects feel it necessary to explain *Alice* and load Mr. Carroll's magical book with all sorts of strange and sometimes unpleasant symbolism. Is it necessary to tear the wings from a butterfly and petals from a rose to see what makes the one soar and the other grow into fragrant beauty?

Now, in the course of this brief research, I've been up and down the stairs twice. For *Alice* dwells on my bedroom bookshelf together with other books very dear to me. There's a Gladys Taber there, a Naomi Mitchison, a Storm Jameson, Mary Webb's *Precious Bane* and, of course, my oldest, small Bible.

It was a source of great happiness to me when I sent my Florida girl grandchild a copy of *Alice* and she fell deeply in love with it. So last time I saw her I gave her my own, which was the "new" edition of 1897. I don't know when I first was able to read it. I began to read at three, but I doubt that, at four, I could have mastered *Alice*. My name is written by me in the front of the book, together with some illegible words. Well, even now, all these years later, most of my written words are illegible. In the back of the book is a list of the publisher's other books. I note I have written "read" beside a number of titles.

My poor pond has been dry for months on end, even the spring and autumn rain and the winter snows did little for it, but I can still walk down to it on a summer evening, fending off gnats and other small winged tormentors, and sit on the lopsided stone bench. There are

157

often children in the playing fields of the school that was built near me some years ago. I can't see the youngsters, but if it's a still night, I can hear them laughing and calling out to one another.

All this month there will be picnics and family and festivities near me. I'll hear music and the ringing sound of horseshoes pitched in someone's yard. There will be children going past on bicycles, some with fishing rods. There are little rivers and ponds bigger than mine not far away; I hope they haven't dried up. I'll go to a picnic or two myself given by the members of the Quota Club, the woman's service organization of which I'm an honorary member, turning up only for parties and picnics.

June, July, and August; these are the months full of light. I read a good deal about Greece and the special light which is shed upon it, and wish I could go there and see for myself. But there's light here, too. I see it slant through my windows; I see it on the ocean and the Sound, I watch it filter through the heavy foliage; gold, tinged with the green of tea leaves. I regard it, as day draws toward its close, casting golden shadows; and at sunset, I see the hot, the brilliant, and then the pastel colors, which are light in the western sky.

I am an impassioned advocate of daylight saving, when, no matter what the sun tells us, there seem to be more hours in a day. I grow quite petulant when it's time to turn the clocks back once more. The only time that daylight saving troubles me is when I have to telephone long distance to a state that doesn't have daylight saving.

Arbitrary time is terribly confusing, at least, it is to me. I suppose I am geared to psychological time and pay very little attention to clocks except when I have an engagement and know that, whatever I may secretly think, most people go by the watches on their wrists or the clocks in their rooms.

I have a fabulous clock given me by friends. Its entire bland face is illuminated; it's a nice soft glow, but definitely there. When it was presented to me, I thought: Oh, no, I have never been able to sleep with a light in the room. Even my electric blanket disturbed me a little when it was turned on and that small red dot showed. At first I turned the clock face away a little; now I turn it so I can see it; I have come to find it companionable. By daylight it has a very gentle pink appearance as if blushing. By night, it is a comfort and security. I can even rise up and grope my way around, without switching on the big lights.

When, last January, the furnace exploded and woke me up, although I didn't know what had awakened me—I'm a long way from the cellar—I instantly looked at the clock. It read two twenty-five, so I was able to establish the time of the explosion. I have since pondered on my good fortune, for normally either the house would have caught fire—and during a blizzard is no time to have a fire, especially in an old frame building—or else there would have been sufficient gas released to put me permanently to sleep.

During that spell of misfortune replete with plumbers, furnace men, and blizzards, my typewriter also went out of whack. Does everything happen in threes?

It was some years ago that I went West to visit Ann, and she took me on a little trip through the Black Hills of South Dakota. We stayed in Deadwood, which was an experience, and it was on the way back that we stopped over for a few days in Denver.

159

Should I get out to Colorado this month, I promise myself I'll not this time be felled by a stupid virus in the Brown Palace Hotel, and if I am there a day or two before going on to the college town in which Ann lives, some sixty-five miles over the mountains, I'll manage a long look at the city itself and maybe even Pike's Peak. I have friends in Denver; one couple who had taken me, my daughter, and a young friend of hers out on the night I was stricken, were so good to me! This time I'd like to show them that I can remain on my feet.

I want to go to Colorado; as far as that goes I want to go to a hundred places: back again to London, and once more to Hawaii and maybe Down Under, to the cities in Europe I've never seen, and to places in the Far East. I'll probably never get to any of them, but I can read about them, see pictures in magazines and on the television screen—and dream a little. Maybe it is as well we can't go everywhere we wish. Many of my friends who have gone by ship around the world on a long cruise come home not remembering completely what they've seen or even where they've been . . . too much has been crowded into a two- or three-month trip. If I were thirty or forty years, and had the time and means, I think I'd take a world cruise to determine, while on it, what I really wanted to see. Then I'd return to this or that place and stay for a week or two or longer and get to know it— unlike the woman on a cruise who stood beside me at a desk in St. Thomas, having come ashore for the day, and asked her companion, "Where are we?" Her friend told her, and the cruiser said, "Oh goodness, I thought we were in St. Thomas *yesterday!*"

I suspect that addicted cruise passengers, after they've taken the same cruise a time or two, don't really know where they are for a day or half a day and perhaps don't care. They return to the ship as birds to the nest, and simply sail on to the next short stop-over.

I was thinking recently that not many people read their own obituaries, at least while still on earth. . . . I know that the late Ernest Hemingway did, at the time he was thought to have been killed in an airplane crash in Africa; and there have been two excellent novels, one of which made a fine motion picture, based on such a theme.

Some time ago I heard from an old school friend with whom I am in touch only at Christmas. What was my astonishment when a letter arrived from her addressed to my family and containing condolences upon my demise. My natural reaction was to borrow a phrase and wire her that the reports of my death were greatly exaggerated. Later, I sat down to figure out how this happened and the only explanation I have is that someone read of Kathleen Norris' death last winter—she was, incidentally, a dear and valued friend of mine—and told someone else who passed it along, and by the time it reached my school friend, it was I, not Mrs. Norris, who had died.

I didn't read Martha's letter, I just glanced at it and became instantly embarrassed. Now I wish I had, but at the time I didn't want to; it was too strange a sensation to read, with my own eyes, pleasant things said about me, but not intended for me to see.

Which reminds me that, at least five years ago, a perfect stranger informed friends of mine that I'd been dead for twenty-two years!

Occurrences like this give one a terrible start. You pinch yourself, wondering, "Lawks a-mercy, can this be I?" Like the old lady in the nursery rhyme who, while she slept, had her petticoats cut off.

Maybe it would be a wonderful idea to write people while they are still upon this earth, or to their families

161

and say you're glad to know them; just as I often think flowers for the living are charming tributes!

The quotation heading this month's chapter is I think delightful, for there is a "live murmur" in every summer day: the murmur of a brook, or the brush of a wing against a bough, the murmur of insects in the tall growing grass, and the leaves in the wind; sometimes it becomes something louder than a murmur—the rumble, for instance, of distant thunder—as far as I am concerned the more distant the better.

But summer *is* a murmur, a sleepy sort of song, a sense of drifting and of dreaming a little; a feeling that time is flowing past, not in haste, but lazily.

Sitting out on the terrace on the still nights not invaded by insect armies, or walking for a little while down my country road—not, alas as country as once it was—I think of friends, nearby and far off, scattered all over the United States or in remote places. I think of those who are dreaming in their own little sections of this small world and of others who have left it, but whom I do not forget. I sometimes believe that when we think with affection of anyone we have ever known, we light a small candle in our hearts, the gleam of which can reach them—either on earth as a sort of mental telepathy or elsewhere—as a tiny light.

I have friends I have not seen for thirty or forty years, but whom I still recall, as they do me; and sometimes we are in touch. There are others who have been gone from this world for a time, and still others whom I have never met but who write me; there are a few who have written to me off and on for over a quarter of a century.

It is a marvelous thing to meet, by chance or design, someone you haven't seen for many years and to be able to pick up the threads and weave them into the old pattern

162

of friendship as if it had never been interrupted. You start where you left off and are the happier for it.

At the beginning of this chapter I spoke of light, and I thought of it again today while I was en route home from a friend's house some twelve miles away. There was a lopsided, early-rising moon in a blue sky. You could just see its pale outline. The moon in the daytime doesn't look like much, but you always know the light is there waiting for the darkness to show itself even though when night falls the moon may be setting. There is always light—in the sun, in the stars, in the moon, and back of the darkest cloud.

I like to think of people, too, as lights; they walk about, solid flesh and blood, but in them there is a spark of the Divine Fire which is in us all. Sometimes it comes to the surface and is recognizable—in someone's eyes, or smile, or the warm tone of a voice. But always it's there, however obscured by the physical self or invisible to another person's lack of vision.

"Let your light so shine before men, that they may see your good works . . ." St. Matthew exhorts. Perhaps we do not always see another person's "good works"; but, if we look for it, we can always see his light.

I have been fortunate. I know people who, just by entering a room, quite unconsciously glorify it with what I call their radiance or incandescence. They simply come in and smile, or maybe say hello, and the light is there and everyone who comes within its range is the better for its shining.

Contrariwise as it says in *Alice*, there are those who can, by entering a room or joining a group, cast a pall of shadow, and this is not conscious either.

Without light, where would we be? How could we

163

grow? Whence obtain warmth? The blind man is, of course, sightless, but he *feels* light; the sunlight warm upon him, or the warmth accorded him by a friendly word, a smile he cannot see but senses.

So now it's summer and there is, much of the time, light all around us, shed from the heavens, reflected upon the waters. Light upon water has a special beauty. And always there is the light of friendship, of understanding and of love, and this is not dependent upon clear skies or a blazing sun.

There used to be a melodramatic old phrase in the stage dramas of my childhood. "Never darken my door again," a stern father would declaim to his erring child. Now we laugh at such phrases, but perhaps we would do well to pray that we may at no time and in no circumstances darken anyone's life, or hopes, or ambitions; we also would do well to pray that we cast no shadows and that we deepen no one's personal darkness by adding our own.

Du Maurier speaks of

> A little warmth, a little light,
> Of love's bestowing . . .

That about sums it up, doesn't it? To give warmth and light in the ordinary everyday ways is not hard, but it is important.

Nowadays we talk a great deal about positive and negative thinking. Maybe it would be simpler to speak of light and of darkness.

Now, a summer month coasts quietly toward yet another of this too short season, one which goes wandering, but with purpose, toward the months of harvest, and a different sort of light.

"Roam on! the light we sought shining still."

MATTHEW ARNOLD

The pause between July and August will be better spent where it's cool. Perhaps you like mountaintops from which you can see great distances. I often think of Whiteface in the Adirondacks; from the summit you can see . . . is it four or five states? The Green Mountains, the White, and even a silver thread which is the St. Lawrence River.

Then there's the ocean. In this country we have a choice of two, the Atlantic or the Pacific. I'd like to be in Hawaii, looking at Diamond Head on the Island of Oahu, or looking seaward from any of the islands. If you prefer the Atlantic, there's the Cape, Long Island, and the east coast of Florida, to name a few, and the coasts of New Jersey and Maine. Oh, the Atlantic is at home on the coasts of many states, northern and southern, from Florida and the Bahamas on past Canada. I have seen it from a lighthouse in Nova Scotia. It is, as are all oceans, a body of water at times destructive and at other times beneficent.

As for the Pacific I've seen it from California, Hawaii, and even Samoa, New Zealand, and Australia. If you are outward bound upon a ship it seems an endless expanse, vast and lonely. Flying is, of course, another matter.

I'd like to sail it again; I remember especially the birds that followed the ship, the flying fish, and at night the phosphorescence.

I know that American Samoa has changed a great deal since the Second World War. I was there in 1939 . . .

165

I don't know how it is now, but then our ship hove to off a reef and the passengers went in to Pago Pago by lighter. This is a beautiful port, mountain-rimmed; the mountain called the Rainmaker is flat on the top and when the clouds gather there, it rains and rains. . . . Out of Samoa's rains the late Somerset Maugham built a short story which became, as every one knows, a celebrated play and motion picture. I recall that we were shown the boardinghouse where Sadie Thompson . . . or rather her prototype lived. Does it still stand? Last winter at the time of our first blizzard, American Samoa had a devastating hurricane and many native dwellings were demolished.

Sailing the North Atlantic, cruise ships can call in at the West Indies, the Bahamas, the Azores, or the Canary Islands, and the Pacific is polka-dotted with islands. Men have longed for a great many years to escape to a lovely, friendly island in the Pacific; not too many have really escaped.

Oceans fascinate me; the changing shore lines, the constant eating away of land by the sea; the silence except in storm. As a child in California, as an adult in Hawaii, I loved the little pools left in the depressions of the rocks or lava, by a receding tide; each was full of colorful tenacious life.

Dunes, wherever they are found, are masterpieces of wind, sea, and water sculpture, altering from one season to the next and on these, too, you will find stubborn life growing; the dune rose, the sturdy beach pea, dusty miller, and the wild grasses.

We are all aware I think of our frail hold on mortal life, but consider the sea shell, the dune plants, and the coral, consider the starfish and the hundreds of sea organisms at the mercy of wind and wave. Think of plants

166

among the rocks, both of seashore or mountain, the delicate determination of trees and bushes, rooted in the smallest crevice, or any fissure which offers a roothold in a little soil. Trees grow out of rocks and often eventually split them. It takes many years, but a tree is patient.

I would suggest a beach, anywhere, somewhat sheltered from the wind but exposed to the sun, from which the resting traveler can see the ceaseless undiminished flow of water and tides, from which he can watch, if he wishes, sunrises, should he face east, or sunset if he is looking toward the west. And of course the lovely dusk, the evening star and the stars which follow it; or the moon casting her silver shadow on the sea.

Sift the sand, fine or coarse, between your fingers, and mark its color, white or pink, or gray or tan. (I remember black sand in Hawaii.) Reflect on how it became what it now is—through the long centuries the pitiless transformation of shells and rocks. There are beaches rimming rivers, lakes, and ponds, as well as ocean beaches formed by sea and weather—the sea is patient and weather unpredictable. The encyclopedia speaks of "Aeolian accumulations" (from Aeolus, the god of the winds). I looked this up because thinking of sand I thought of deserts . . . they are formed by dust, tiny particles of soil and even sand grains transported by wind.

Sand is everywhere, in our soil, at the bottom of bodies of water and blown across plains. Dunes are found in many places too, on ocean beaches and, I just remembered, Lake Michigan. And there are "wandering dunes," a term which has always delighted me.

But the one I have selected where we now can sit and dream a little won't wander; it will, however, change. If we return next year we will find it altered—lower, per-

167

haps longer, wider, or higher, and the shape we remember shifted, even if a very little.

If my sister were with us, she would have brought an elaborate picnic basket and perhaps even a pot of tea protected by the quilted cozy. I don't know at what time of day we are pausing, maybe at sunrise, maybe lunch or teatime, perhaps even supper. If supper, Esther would have a beach fire going. Actually there are few things more delightful than beach fires.

Some time ago my friend, Father Gilbert, sent me from Maryland a small leaflet, and on it is a sketch of water, sky, a boat and a solitary man, in blues and greens, and, a prayer.

I have it taped to the upright eyeglass case on my desk and look at it a dozen times a day. The few words are called "Breton Fisherman's Fishermen's Prayer" and they read:

> Dear God be good to me,
> The sea is so wide
> And my boat is so small.

This is a prayer for us all, for the world is a wide sea and the vessel of our lives is small and vulnerable and there are reefs and rocks, tides and storms which we must encounter.

But on the wide sea there is light as we go on to another month together.

August

". . . and dream
Of waves, flowers, clouds, woods, rocks, and
all that we
Read in their smiles, and call reality."

SHELLEY

This is a lazy month, a languid handful of days. Traffic is as insistent as ever and vacationers wear themselves out, swimming, sailing, fishing, climbing mountains and exercising on tennis courts and golf links, going to parties, and giving them, and shopping frantically—if possible, on bad days, which are not beach days, as they say on the Cape—so they won't miss one ray of sunshine. They become fat or thin, tanned or lobster red; and are happy. But August is close to September and in September the schools reopen.

Yet despite the vacationers' activities or even the backyard tumult of stay-at-home people, laziness prevails, even if not physically, for it is necessary to pack the remaining summer days into your trunk, stowing the time away, filling every corner, and maybe even sitting on the lid to close summer in. But laziness is in the air, it affects the trees and the birds, and even little rivers seem to run more slowly. Only the sea is unaffected.

I do not know whether I'll be away part of this month or not, but if I'm home, it will be a good time to work, although I may make the heat an excuse to stay away from the typewriter. When I have plenty of free time and work is the answer to long-drawn-out hours, I am most apt not to work at all, or not very much. Possibly I work better under pressure because when I first began to write I was faced with impossible deadlines. I used to ask editors "When will you want this?" and they often replied, quite seriously "oh, the week before last!"

We are all very much aware that the era in which we are living is complicated by tensions, pressure, and fear, and I often talk about these, privately and publicly and even suggest time-tested remedies with which to over-come them. I admit I don't often take my own medicine. However, as always, there is another side to the coin. I don't recommend tension at any time, but pressure can serve a good purpose if you are as naturally lazy as I. Left to my own sweet will, without the deadlines set me by relentless editors, I would have accomplished very little. Fear too is salutary, up to a point. Without fear, few of us could long endure upon this earth. A certain amount—call it caution or realism, if you'd rather—is necessary; otherwise who would cross a street or face any physical crisis in safety?

Long ago, when first we moved to the country, the streets of the nearby village and the back roads were not overburdened with traffic. They are now. So you wait and wait and then make a dash for it, and I dislike dashing. We used to leave our doors unlocked then, too. I haven't for many years, which is caution, a spin-off of fear.

This month is, as was last, a time of sudden thunder storms and I don't like them. I run about disconnecting appliances and closing doors and windows, whether I suffocate or not. All this is part of fear of fire, living as I once did and do again in a frame house with very big trees close to it. My father when I first began to worry about storms—I was sixteen I think—used to march me out on the front porch of his country house and say "But you never see the bolt that hits you." This was cold comfort to me, and actually I am not afraid of being struck by lightning—I've been hit too often psychologically and emotionally speaking—I'm afraid for the house and the trees.

It is essential for man to walk delicately in this world which people now refer to as a jungle, for while civilization has conquered the land and learned to forecast and calculate natural disasters, chart the winds, and sometimes soothe the seas and to invade Outer Space, it has also brought some very unpleasant aspects, not always confined to big cities which are, paradoxically, the uncivilized side of civilization. Here caution becomes vital. Primitive man had strange gods to fear, he sought for shelter during storms, he was terrified by an eclipse of the sun, he had animals to contend with, and also his neighbor. We aren't afraid of eclipses although some people regard them as trouble breeders, but we haven't progressed as far as we believe, have we? We are still seeking shelter, although from different dangers, still avoiding attacks—if not from wild animals—and still fearing our fellow man.

If caution includes a certain amount of fear, we should not feel guilty. Anxiety is something else again, and usually operates in the field of material need and in that of our relationships with other people.

I sometimes wish I'd been born in the 1870's. That period had many drawbacks as historians are quick to point out, but I think of it as basically slow-moving and quieter, and if you couldn't leap into an automobile or fly off to dinner in London or sail the Atlantic in less than five days, if you couldn't get to a business engagement several hundred miles away in a few hours or go calling on a remote relative, in a sense you had more freedom. Perhaps that was because communications, as we know them, had not yet been developed and the people who lived at that time were not bombarded, day and night, by news, rumors, and the reports of distant tragedies in our country and other countries. All they had were newspapers . . . no telephones, nor radios, nor television, no reporters on the spot, no news analysts. I presume the average person had no personal sense of belonging to any part of the larger world beyond his own community and state.

Appliances didn't go out of order either, there were none, such as we now have. Oh, wells ran dry and windmills were static on a breathless day, but you couldn't talk about power failure. I admit I would not care to return to the day of the oil lamp—I've cleaned some in my time—or the washboard. But I wouldn't mind the horse and buggy!

Yet I suppose that the years of my own life have been as interesting and exciting in many ways as any in recorded history. All eras have had wars, catastrophes, epidemics, and uncertainties. But during mine I've lived to see the almost incredible advances in the sciences—in engineering, medicine, communications. I remember

172

the first automobile in which I rode as a passenger. It took three days to get to a destination that now takes a few hours. I remember trains which took a week to cross the continent. And I saw the development of the airplane. And all this progress is still going on; every day you hear of a step forward. Just today I read of the new-found medical ability to heal unborn children.

Always I have lived in a time of great men and women and I have even known a few of them. There have been great people in every era of course, but as one looks back, it would seem that the right person or persons for that particular period appeared at the right time.

I have no serious quarrel with progress really and if I think that the seventies or the eighties were more peaceful, I'm probably wrong; but I'm certain the pace was slower and that there wasn't as much noise.

The plan of Nature is progress and for any progress mankind must pay a price. It is quite evident to me that man must pay for everything except for the natural beauty of the landscape, which, if he is fortunate enough to live where it still exists, is free. Beauty has always existed and always will. Man has destroyed much of it, but he can never destroy all. The oceans are unchanged and the rivers still flow, even though some of them are laden with pollution, and some overflow, and others are less brimful than they were. The mountains stand. Man has made changes, he builds highways, cuts down trees, deflects a river's course as well as poisons it, yet beauty remains.

Therefore, I think we should take time to enjoy what we can see of it.

There are not many geographical frontiers left in this country. . . . I often think that if I were a young man with no ties nor attachments, I'd head for Aus-

173

tralia; that's a big, wide, wonderful country where there are still frontiers; there are friendly and interesting people, strange animals and gorgeous varied scenery and certainly a varied climate.

Every time any frontier is tamed or an advance made in the conquering of disease or a brilliant invention is successful someone always says, "There are *no* more frontiers." It's not true. Maybe there aren't many natural ones in these United States; but there are other places; and we have just begun to know something about Outer Space. There are no more covered wagons, but there are always new goals. Much of the world has embarked upon projects designed to create better lives for the less fortunate, to enlist in the age-old battle for justice, and to reach the age-old goal of peace and brotherhood. The world and all its people cannot afford to stand still and rest upon the laurels so far achieved. More and more we learn not to be complacent and indifferent. Perhaps at one time indifference was just a matter of not caring much about someone who didn't live next door or move in your own close circle. Today everyone lives next door to everyone else and what affects your neighbor, thousands of miles away, must eventually affect you.

Indifference, I believe, is a major sin. I've spoken of the bygone time when, owing to lack of communications people were more indifferent, or perhaps it's more accurate to say less disturbed by the world's difficulties than we now are. I suppose it wasn't really indifference, but ignorance. No one can plead that now.

Civilization has its drawbacks but also its advantages, and ordinary, commonsense caution its uses. The great enduring qualities have been inherent in man since his emergence from the cave; trust and hope, and love. There have always been people, the pioneers in compassion, who cared deeply about what happened to others. Today most of us care about what happens not only next door but to unknown families leagues away. Yet before us were those who also cared, without exposure to our present knowledge, or the instant reporting to which we are accustomed. There have for a long time been missionaries at home, as well as abroad.

My older daughter recently erupted into the study, having come down from her upstate home to pay an unannounced call. She told me it was hot—something which I really knew, and that therefore she'd make iced tea. "Where is the mint?" she demanded. "Courtesy of Gussie, there's some in the ice box," I answered but when she asked what happened to the mint bed which used to flourish near the kitchen porch, I couldn't tell her as I haven't the slightest idea.

Presently she will bring in a frosty pitcher and two glasses, but my glass will be innocent of ice; ice and I are not compatible. All you have to do for me is to put the pitcher—or my individual glass—in the refrigerator for a while. My sister makes the world's best iced tea, in great quantities and stores it. It keeps. It took her a while to realize that while I do not drink as many glasses as she does, I lower the level in her quart bottles faster than she, as her glass is always choked with ice.

A while back I spoke of appliances. There are a number which I don't think I could do without, although had I lived before they were invented, I would not have missed them. I remember our first telephone in the country; it hung on the wall and you cranked it furiously, and usually besought someone to get off the line. Our first radio was a crystal set, but we progressed to one which had a morning-glory sort of horn, like the old phonographs, and then to a huge cabinet affair—very different

175

from the transistor which fits into the palm of my hand. I also remember the first motion picture I saw—it was all motion, I assure you—and the gradual advance to the good non-leaping silent pictures, and then to the talking ones (when I first saw and heard them, I firmly prophesied "This will not last"), and to the first picture in Technicolor.

Sometimes I wonder what I did with one short-wave radio. I used to listen to it by the hour, eavesdropping on ship-to-shore conversations and trying to tune in strange countries and languages.

When we bought our first freezer—we still have it, though it's not as convenient, I believe, as the new ones—I thought man had reached the end of invention. He hasn't. The comparatively new icebox from which Hervey took the mint is a reliable presence in the kitchen, but I've seen some in television commercials which seem to do everything but talk and make your bed.

Television. I saw it first in a shop window, and then at a friend's home. Now, I'm asked, "Don't you have color TV yet?" I haven't; I'm happy with what I have, at least for the time being.

I am writing this on a typewriter which came on the market less than five years ago and was the last word in typewriters. Lately it's been emotional, and has given me trouble, a few weeks ago, a few days ago and today. It has been diagnosed by experts and they have gravely informed me that the prognosis is dire.

My machine is "obsolete."

I am aware that in the cases of planes and battleships one reads that one or the other is now obsolete (after a short time), but the term never reached me really until now.

It is fortunate that, at age five, the human being is not

176

considered obsolete, or I'd have to retire a grandchild or two. Even at my age I don't think that I'm a museum piece, although I'm sure my younger friends and relatives secretly believe so when I fail to keep up with current tastes in music, Pop art, the newest in literature. I am confused by what's "in" and what isn't, to say nothing of Camp, and the wildly athletic dances of the moment, during which partners appear oblivious of each other's presence. Well, those who once danced the minuet were physically separated although they at least, gingerly touched hands, and were somewhat more stately. . . .

There. I've had two long telephone conversations and made a great many illegible corrections on my copy and silently prayed that the unfortunate typist who has to decipher them will be given strength and heightened intuition. During this time out, the typewriter took a nap or went for a refreshing walk, for when I returned to the desk it did not scream, bark, or bounce, but stood still doing absolutely nothing.

Perhaps when I go to bed, the typewriter—to which I'm so attached that its nervous breakdown saddens me— will take a long, quiet rest and decide it's well enough to operate, come morning. I hope it doesn't stay awake and dream up, in malice, some new antic. Lacking the gloomy diagnostician, all I can do in the home-nursing department is to pause at the end of a page and permit the patient to rest.

Something will come along to balance this difficulty, as a year ago this month life, or fate, took away with one hand, and gave with the other.

The deprivation was a staggering blow, unexpected and without any warning, in my professional life. The writer becomes, of course, accustomed to disappointments

177

and rejections over the years, just as anyone has to in any field whatsoever. But this was different. It was as if I were on a smoothly running train with a destination years away and it suddenly stopped, and the conductor announced, "This is as far as we go. All out!" Aside from material loss, the shock to one's professional pride (call it vanity, if you will; perhaps it is) is painful.

On the other hand, and on the very same day my Florida grandchildren and their mother arrived for a short visit. The children had never been north, except the little girl but, as she was about six months old at the time, and came to this house to be baptized I doubt that she recalls it. They saw the Fair before they came to me, and went by bus to Rhode Island to an uncle's, and while they were here with me we had a family picnic, brimming with relatives, friends, children, and offering all the things they liked best to eat and drink. Gussie and her husband, Lawrence, outdid themselves and the evening was fine. And the next day, before they returned home, the two youngsters were given their first watches by their godparents. So, deprivation on the one hand, delight on the other.

That's why I say, as I prepare to rest the typewriter again: "Something good has to happen."

August, like all the other months, is a remembering month for me. I sometimes wish I could forget dates . . . there are cards you can buy, birthday greetings, which say "sorry I forgot," but I keep on consulting little books in which I've noted everyone's birthday or anniversary. No, I really don't mean that. I like remembering but according to the perpetual balance there are also unhappy dates to recall.

Writing this so early in the month I still do not know where I'll be next week or the week after, but I'm certain that, when the next month comes, I'll be starting another book, a novel this time, provided this typewriter holds out or a new one comes my way.

Last spring in Florida I hoped for a magnificent inspiration. I had the theme for a novel. I've had it for years, and even the title, but how to shape it eluded me, and I did not believe I could handle it with even moderate success. So I sat in the Florida sun, often alone, or out on the balcony of the hotel room at night and waited for the lightning to strike—not, this time, the brilliant silent partner of a noisy thunder storm but the dazzling illumination of an idea. Perhaps I'm not receptive when I'm idle and enjoying myself. I know that two pleasant ideas—or the beginnings of them—once came to me when I was taking a very hurried bath.

But I couldn't sit quietly in a tub all during my Florida visit.

This is going to be a thirteen-month book. I like the number thirteen, a whimsey I shared with my father. I also like to fashion a month from whole cloth. I recall again the program called "That Was the Week That Was." So, this will be a month that hasn't been and which I've not yet lived, nor has anyone else, for that matter.

It will have to be a short chapter (*"Ole!"* says the typewriter), for nothing can go into it but hope and remembrance of bygone days.

While I write of my thirteenth month I cannot write of plans other than those for work and even that may have to be postponed. I can't talk about the weather, except of that of vanished Septembers because how do I know what the weather will be like.

But at the moment it is still August, the drowsy and dreamy month, despite the activities of those of us who

179

romp through it; the month when office workers home from holiday wish they hadn't returned and move closer to the air conditioning, the month which warns us of things to come by suddenly producing a cool night after a hot day. This is the last month which is entirely summer—there are only two, really July and August, for most of June is spring.

This August has been generous with moonlight, a full moon on the first day, and another on the next to last.

"Summer's lease," said Shakespeare, in a sonnet, "hath all too short a date." I cannot wholly agree. There are parts of the world where it's summer all year round. The advantages of eternal summer are obvious, in a practical sense; no seasonal clothes, nothing to store away in mothballs, no furnaces to worry about, no impassable roads, except during the big rains, swimming, if water's handy, every day and the ability to live outdoors most of the time. But all this wouldn't compensate me for the surprises of four seasons . . . unpleasant sometimes, but never monotonous.

The typewriter is beginning to buck again and scream a little, so I'll go upstairs, look for my evening star and think with John Keats, "Bright star, would I were steadfast as thou art."

"There is a pleasure in the pathless woods, . . ."

LORD BYRON

Between each of the months we have looked for roads and paths, for mountaintops and seashore, and walked

180

awhile, or rested. But now between last month and the one I shall imagine there need be no path at all toward the journey's end.

We have been somewhere, and on familiar ground; now we look ahead to somewhere else, which is not familiar at all but, one day, will be.

I cannot forecast, as those who write proper almanacs do, or calculate the rising of sun and stars and moons; nor can I foretell events. Even almanacs can't, except such events as occur in nature. I know only that every day, in every month, is a closed book until it dawns, and is a miniature new year and a beginning again.

Astrologers, charting the courses, implications, and influences of the stars forecast for the individual person the months not yet at hand. But I'm no astrologer.

So walk with me a little while in the pathless woods and reflect upon the unknown.

A large part of the excitement and challenge of living is that the past is gone, the present here, and the future masked. Yet the three tenses are inextricably one, for yesterday has bearing on today and today upon tomorrow. It was George Eliot who said, "Our deeds still travel with us from afar."

Every year contains something of all the years we have so far lived and something of the years which remain to us. I have heard children ask, "When is tomorrow?" and also, "What happened to yesterday?" The answer to each question is that yesterday and tomorrow are bound up in today.

The calendar states hard cold facts, and one cannot dispute them. But only in the outward sense does man live by a calendar; actually he lives both backward and forward.

I suppose that the truly happy man brings tools forged

181

yesterday for use today and tomorrow and in this way shapes, as nearly as he can, his destiny.

I find myself enchanted by Byron's "pathless woods," and it isn't hard to visualize them: tall, crowding trees, between which you make your way; the scent of earth and foliage and of evergreens. And, looking up, a patch of bright blue sky. This seems to me as restful as the remembered or imaginary garden I spoke of some time ago. And, unless a leaf fell or a bird sang, there would be silence in the woods except for one's own footsteps which would, I dare say, be hushed also.

In the woods there must be a sense that time has ceased and that for a moment we pause on the edge of some extraordinary discovery, that for the space of a heartbeat we are close to knowledge, on the verge of the solution to all problems, on the threshold of an answer.

Pathless woods, steeped in peace and towering between heaven and earth would, I think, have that answer waiting for us if we were receptive enough to hear it.

This is also true of everyday life when we are walking familiar ways, for moments of revelation are not confined to the quiet hours or the daydream. If, in our relationships with others, we are able even occasionally to become receptive so that we can listen with the ears of the heart as well as with the physical ear and the mind, we often find ourselves, not on the verge of knowledge but entering into knowledge itself and understanding.

So much is said, everyone almost talks all the time, but more than is spoken is left unuttered. It is then, if you permit it, that the heart hears. You can learn as much about a friend or a stranger from what they do not say as from what is expressed in words; you learn more of their anxieties, sorrows, and inner happiness by listening with the heart than in any other way.

182

Here in the woods perhaps we can listen with the heart and with the spirit, and hear the trees speak of growth, and the earth of seeds and silence, and looking up to the sky, hear sunlight singing.

September

"The day becomes more solemn and serene
When noon is past—there is a harmony
In autumn, and a lustre in its sky,
Which through the summer is not heard or seen,
As if it could not be, as if it had not been!"

SHELLEY

So now we arrive at September, a little ahead of schedule.
And as long as I am going to shape it to my fancy, I shall
see to it that this custom-made month will not fetch with
it any of the unwanted surprises which September-for-
real can bring. We are not to have hurricanes, not anywhere, not in the South or North, not East or West, or
indeed in any part of the world. I will not tolerate earth-
quakes or tidal waves or epidemics or vacillating weather.
In this September there must be warm days, but not too
warm. Too often Labor Day arrives with a heat wave and

sometimes it continues and the children, mourning summer, are no longer on holiday but back at school. Thunderstorms will not occur, and the nights must be cool for sleeping. If you like a touch of frost to sparkle on ground and grass as you drink your morning tea or coffee, I shall contrive that it be light and transient, and do no harm to the September wild and garden flowers.

Also, over the long and perilous Labor Day weekend, I insist that in this made-to-order month all accidents on the road must be minor.

Is it too much to ask of my imagination that it conceive that the new fall season of television be more satisfying to the eye, ear, and mind than it usually is? I'd keep the good programs (regardless of ratings) and those which I, selfishly, prefer, and cancel out the unpleasant and absurd, and bring on those which are not only educational and factual but beautiful as well. Documentaries, not shallow but substantial, which will bring us into other countries, through which we can climb mountains and sail rivers, and into cities we've not seen and deserts we may never see. I would have great plays and great actors; and the reading of poetry. I would also have laughter, not the laughter educed by flung pies or embarrassing situations—all of which have a trace of cruelty —but honest laughter devoid of malice, or the secret satisfaction of watching someone make a spectacle of himself —the kind of laughter which rises from the heart and also warms it.

There's too little honest laughter on or off television screens. But then, of course, I remind myself that people do not always laugh at the same things; what seems comic to one may appear tragic to another.

As in any September, most people are back at work, so I would not only have the outdoor climate pleasant but

185

the indoor, and that goes for encounters with fellow workers, superiors, subordinates, and the passer-by.

I think that this month I will, by some alchemy, have people walk through it with courtesy. Honest courtesy is as rare as honest laughter, and it, too, springs from the heart.

It seems to have become very difficult genuinely to smile, to say, "I'm sorry," to step aside and wait for someone else to be served; to say "Thank you" and "Please" and "How are you this morning?" That's usually because we forget, or sometimes because we hurry. But we needn't hurry through this month. We can take time; we can make time, for the amenities; and for looking back and also ahead, and for the quiet moments we promise ourselves every month and rarely manage to achieve. And we can spend more of September's hours in prayer than we usually do.

Prayer is thought, and thought is the most powerful weapon any one of us has at his command. "For as he thinketh in his heart, so is he" we are warned in Proverbs. The unknown writer who set down these words was referring to an evil man. But it is true of all of us, good, bad, and indifferent; as we think, so are we.

I cannot truthfully tell you that I am a faithful practitioner of positive thinking. I know that I should be according to the psychologists, but I'm not, however much I try. Doubt creeps in, worry, or anticipation of something that may never come to pass. On the other hand I don't *want* to think so positively all the time that I become aloof, and unaffected by other people's distress. I have friends who, in talking to others, apparently listening to their difficulties, lower a curtain of indifferent glass. The bullet that has wounded someone else can't penetrate to the listener; that sort of glass is shatterproof.

186

If it's negative thinking that calls out empathy, I'm all for it, in that aspect; for I do not believe that to suffer with, and for, others weakens you; it is a form of sharing.

Thought—the thoughts for others, the prayer which is not merely a beseeching—any thought, actually, travels far faster than the speed of light. I have said before that if I think of a distant place, I am there before the clock ticks; or if I think of people, I am with them, for the moment. Shakespeare's Puck could "put a girdle round about the earth in forty minutes," but we can do it in the time it takes to think.

Thought has no limitation, other than those we impose upon our thinking. It can heal, it can comfort, it can bring light into darkness. Oddly enough we can sometimes do for others, through thought, what we cannot always do for ourselves.

You do not know me, yet you have been with me on this small journey through a year and a month. So, I think of you, whoever you may be, as I set down these words on a typewriter which has, for the moment, decided to behave.

I would rather have one good and loving thought directed toward me than a thousand material gifts; for the gifts won't last, but the thought that finds its destination endures.

We often say, usually with regret, "I spoke—or acted—without thinking." Well, not entirely, really, for some kind of thought had to be there or we couldn't have spoken or acted at all. What we mean is, we did not think clearly; we did not take the time.

There's a little bit from *Alice in Wonderland* which we would do well to remember. It goes like this:

"Really, now you ask me," said Alice, very much confused. "I don't think—"

"Then you shouldn't talk," said the Hatter.

Of course, it was rude of him to interrupt, but he was on the right track.

Thought has everything to offer; it is defense, it can also be attack—an attack upon the things which diminish the spirit and drain the emotions; and a defense against those things. It can always create, for all creativity springs from thought and it can re-create, in every sense of the word, not only the spirit and the physical self but the scenes of the past, the remembrance of love, and all experience. The good and loving thought can work wonders and perform miracles.

It has its other side; we call it "negative." Yet there are always two sides; there is light and darkness; good and evil; strength and weakness. And all our thinking is a mixture of these. But because I believe in people I also believe that the good is heavier in the scale than the evil, perhaps because I've been fortunate enough to see more of one than of the other.

How often have people said to you and to me, half laughing, "Send me a good thought." They may be going to face an unpleasantness or departing in a plane or on a ship; they may just be troubled about something minor. And we answer, "Of course," but I wonder how often we follow through.

So in this little September and in the actual one which will soon follow, I hope I can think less of myself and more of others, as constructively as my own limitations permit.

September is still summer. Autumn—despite Shelley's words at the beginning of this chapter—will not be with us until the twenty-third, at an hour in the morning when I trust I'll still be asleep. But before autumn formally begins in every proper September, including this fanciful one, the leaves will start to turn; one here, and another there. I look for the first autumnal flush in the swamp maples and dogwoods and on my cork tree or burning bush, which will suddenly exhibit a shocking-pink leaf or two.

This is a lovely month, even when it arrives in reality, and is not as I have here composed it.

Cranberries will be harvested on Cape Cod, oysters are in season, and people go crabbing in cold salt waters. The full harvest moon will rise in molten gold and cool into silver. There are many saints' days in September and various states will celebrate their own holidays. On the fifteenth there is Rosh Hashana and on the twenty-fourth, as autumn comes quietly in, Yom Kippur.

Gussie just came in to announce, "It's almost supper time," then inquire, "You reading the almanac again?"

Of course, what would I do without it, me—myself—who cannot keep engagements straight, or a check book either? So if now and then I make an error, it's not the almanac's fault, but mine. I have reached the stage where my reading glasses balk at fine, crowded print, so I remove them and peer with my own naked, nearsighted, astigmatic eyes and often misread.

Once upon a time I wrote a period novel and to guide me in world occurrences I used a dictionary of events. One of my editors caught an error of a whole year; I had just misread the page and date.

I can console myself only by saying sadly: "No one is perfect!"

I'd planned to write a little verse at the end of this journey but in the last few months it seems to me that I have been writing reams of rhyming couplets or, as a friend unkindly put it, doggerel. This was done for fun and other people's amusement. Now when I think of rhyme I find myself "going to the doggerel" again, which is a very bad pun. I hope I'm around when my son-in-law reads this. He's an inveterate punster no matter how often I tell him I don't like puns.

So what about blank verse? I've always been very fond of it.

Poetry, light, lyric, profound—has always been a source of delight to me since first I discovered it. My father loved it; he wrote good light verse, in his younger days, and sometimes in letters sent me when I was away from home. School gave me poetry in the early grades, and I was fortunate enough to have at boarding school an inspired teacher who, when we studied Shakespeare, permitted us, on spring days, to sit out under the trees and read aloud, each in her selected role. There was a time when I began to write in verse, and a while, a very long period, when it was impossible for me to write any at all! Then, for a short time I returned to it; but now no more, except at the end of some of my books and the "doggerel."

There have also been times when I couldn't bear to read poetry; and times when no other reading gave me anything at all.

So now I'll find someone else's poetry with which to end September. Thank you for being with me, as I traveled through the baker's dozen months. If you have left me sometime during it, I cannot fault you for it. Not everyone enjoys another person's travels, whether in books or on the home motion-picture screens or in albums. But even if you've gone just a little way with me and not long enough to reach my second September, thank you.

This is by George John Whyte-Melville:

> The swallows are making them ready to fly,
> Wheeling out on a windy sky:
> Goodbye, Summer, goodbye, goodbye.

Reprise

(FOR R.E.B.)

Lines written on the back of an airplane ticket

In some indefinite and unknown hour
By day or night, a journey will begin
Which I shall make, as swift as thought, alone;
And I must travel light, discarding all
Impedimenta; useless, clogging weight
Long since paid for in full.

                          I'll take, instead,
Love, given and received, and memory
Of every beauty seen, and felt, and touched.
Thus, made my own.

                          I cannot specify
My destination, but, as God is kind
It may be that I'll reach my Evening Star
And see it wholly; radiant as Grace;
As Mercy, pure; as Love, compassionate.